Iron Horses in the Valley

The Valley and Shenandoah Valley Railroads 1866–1882

John R. Hildebrand

Published by

 BURD STREET PRESS
SHIPPENSBURG, PENNSYLVANIA

THE HISTORY MUSEUM AND HISTORICAL SOCIETY OF WESTERN VIRGINIA
ROANOKE, VIRGINIA

THE SALEM HISTORICAL SOCIETY
SALEM, VIRGINIA
2001

This Burd Street Press publication
was printed by
Beidel Printing House, Inc.
63 West Burd Street
Shippensburg, PA 17257-0152 USA

The acid-free paper used in this book meets the guidelines for permanence and durability of the Committee on Production Guidelines for Book Longevity of the Council on Library Resources.

For a complete list of available publications
please write
Burd Street Press
Division of White Mane Publishing Company, Inc.
P.O. Box 152
Shippensburg, PA 17257-0152 USA

Library of Congress Cataloging-in-Publication Data

Hildebrand, John R., 1926-
    Iron horses in the valley : the Valley and Shenandoah Valley Railroads, 1866–1882 / by
John Hildebrand.
        p. cm.
    Includes bibliographical references and index.
    ISBN 1-57249-232-5 (alk. paper)
    1. Shenandoah Valley Railroad--History. 2. Valley Railroad (Va.)--History. 3.
Railroads--Virginia--History. I. History Museum and Historical Society of Western
Virginia. II. Salem Historical Society (Va.) III. Title.

TF25.S48 H55 2001
385'.09755'9--dc21
                                                                00-068902

Dedication

This book is dedicated to the memory of Horace Grover Fralin, 1927–1993. He was a man of many talents, first as an electrical engineer, then as a builder, developer, and business man.

More importantly, Horace was an outstanding citizen. During World War II he served in the United States Navy. Throughout his business career he maintained an active interest in the governance of Roanoke city and the Commonwealth of Virginia, serving on numerous boards and commissions.

Horace's greatest contributions were in the areas of education, history, and the arts. He shared his knowledge, talents, and resources with Virginia Tech, his alma mater, Roanoke College, the Art Museum of Western Virginia, the Jefferson Center, Explore Park, and many other institutions and organizations.

The Horace G. Fralin Charitable Trust continues to make his influence felt throughout western Virginia. Its grants and contributions continue to benefit and advance the liberal arts.

It was my privilege to know Horace as a friend, high school classmate, and college roommate. It is my hope that this book will, in some small measure, serve as a reminder of his lifetime of service and dedication to city, state, and nation.

Horace Grover Fralin was truly a Renaissance man.

Contents

List of Illustrations and Maps... vii

Acknowledgments ix

Author's Personal Note.. xi

    I. The Genesis of the Valley and Shenandoah Valley Railroads...................... 1

    II. Big Lick Forever? 14

    III. A History of the Shenandoah Valley Railroad, 1867–1882 19

    IV. A History of the Valley Railroad, 1866–1881 47

    V. Building the Valley Railroad, Staunton to Salem.................................... 68

Appendix: Valley Railroad Atlas and Photographs, Lexington to Salem 89

Notes... 117

Bibliography 122

Index 125

Illustrations and Maps

ILLUSTRATIONS

Fort Defiance Depot 4
Bridge over Middle River 4
Bridge over Mill Creek 5
Lexington Station and Depot 5
Thomas A. Scott 8
John Work Garrett 8
William Mahone 8
William Milnes, Jr. 26
Frederick J. Kimball 31
Shenandoah Valley Construction Train 34
1881 Shenandoah Valley Railroad Stock Certificate 44
Old 199 56
Engineers in Camp 71
Claibourne Rice Mason 74
Making an Embankment 80
Building a Masonry Arch 81
Walker May 85
Valley Railroad, Lexington to Salem .... Appendix, 105–16

MAPS

Virginia Railroads, 1872 9
Alternate Routes, Shenandoah Valley Mainline into Big Lick and Bonsack 40
Valley Railroad Atlas, Lexington to Salem .... Appendix, 91–103

Acknowledgments

The development of the Valley and Shenandoah Valley Railroads was a part of the tremendous expansion of the nation's railroad system that occurred during the decades following the Civil War. Although these two railroads were only a small part of the nationwide effort, a history of their development over a 15-year period required the assistance, guidance, and resources of many individuals and libraries. Without the support of friends, librarians, and family members this book would not have been written.

The principal source of research material for the two railroad companies was the collections of two libraries. The Hays T. Watkins Research Library at the B&O Railroad Museum in Baltimore, Maryland, and its archivist, Ms. Ann Calhoun, provided the information used in preparing the history of the Valley Railroad. The Special Collections Department of the University Libraries at Virginia Tech, Blacksburg, Virginia, provided the information on which the history of the Shenandoah Valley Railroad was based. Ms.

Jan Carlton and the staff of this department were most helpful in retrieving the applicable records. I appreciate very much the courtesies extended by each library and its staff.

The assistance of Carol Tuckwiler and Brenda Findley at the Virginia Room of the Roanoke Public Library was most helpful in arranging library loans for many of the references used in preparing the book. The Reference Librarians of the Library of Virginia were also helpful in making available the reports of the Virginia Railroad Commissioner. The Law Libraries of Roanoke City and Roanoke County were likewise valuable sources of information.

Friends also played important roles. John Streat of Richmond helped with research at the Library of Virginia. Lon Savage and Don Piedmont, both outstanding writers, reviewed and critiqued initial drafts. George Kegley, an authority on the history of the Roanoke Valley and southwestern Virginia, reviewed the manuscript at several stages of its development. He offered many comments and suggestions which improved and clarified the text. His help was invaluable and greatly appreciated. Melissa Wade edited the initial drafts. Doug Kayton prepared the portrait of Claibourne R. Mason, and Bob Fry developed the sketches illustrating the methods used in building masonry arches. Mary Crockett Hill, director of the Salem Museum, and Jennifer Joiner, friend and neighbor, assisted with the design of the book cover.

The contributions of my former partners and associates at Hayes, Seay, Mattern and Mattern, Architects and Engineers, must also be recognized. They made available the firm's data processing and reproduction facilities in preparing the book's maps and photographs for publication, an invaluable service.

My family's help was immeasurable. Daughters, granddaughter, and sons-in-law were involved. Martha Karen, Bob and Meg Sherwood; Caroline and Jay Cochrane; and Sarah Caldwell provided instruction and insight into the intricacies of the word processor and the creation of files for the storage and printing of the manuscript at various stages of development. Finally, the book would not have been possible without the patient and understanding support of my dear wife, Tootie. I am most thankful that she endured my many hours at the word processor with patience and understanding and helped with the photography and research at the Watkins Library.

Author's Personal Note

I cannot adequately express my appreciation to the organizations and individuals whose financial contributions made publication of *Iron Horses in the Valley* possible. It was only through the support of these sponsors that my efforts in writing this book were brought to fruition. With deepest gratitude I acknowledge their gracious help.

The Horace G. Fralin Charitable Trust

The History Museum and Historical Society of Western Virginia

The Salem Historical Society

Virginia Section, American Society of Civil Engineers

Graham White Manufacturing Company

Natalie Roberts Foster Lemon

J. Oliver Stein

John Pilcher Bradshaw, Jr.

R. W. Thompson

Sam and Lorinda Lionberger

Stan Lanford

Chapter I
The Genesis of the Valley and Shenandoah Valley Railroads

INTRODUCTION

A journey on US Route 11 and Interstate Route 81 from Harrisonburg south to Salem can be intriguing for the historian, particularly one with an interest in railroads. The journey will reveal traces of the old Valley Railroad, organized in 1866.

Beginning at Harrisonburg and proceeding south to Staunton, the existing tracks can be seen at many locations. At Fort Defiance, just east of Route 11, one of the original depots, an attractive frame structure, remains. Just north of Verona, where Route 11 crosses Middle River, one of the original bridges can be seen. It was constructed in 1872, using wrought-iron girders supported by masonry piers.

Between Staunton and Lexington along southbound Route 81, a four-span masonry viaduct over Mill Creek is located at milepost 219. From this point into Lexington, a close observation of the countryside on either side of Route 81 will reveal traces of the old roadbed and remains of other masonry structures.

At Lexington, just west of Nelson Street (US Route 60) and the Washington and Lee University campus, the original Lexington station and depot has been attractively restored.

The largest concentration of the Valley Railroad's remains is located between Lexington and Natural Bridge along Route 610, the Plank Road. This area can be reached by following Routes 251 and 764 south from Lexington. After crossing Buffalo Creek and proceeding south on Route 610 until it intersects Route 11 south of Natural Bridge, masonry bridge abutments, masonry arches and boxes in different stages of completion and evidences of the original roadbed can be seen.

Continuing south along Route 11 into Botetourt County, a 12-foot arch is located about 0.7 mile south of the Cedar Bluff Church, north of the I-81 interchange for Arcadia. Highway construction has destroyed all other evidences of the Valley Railroad in Botetourt County, except in the vicinity of Tinker Mountain.

Other remaining evidences of the Valley Railroad are found between Salem and the Roanoke County-Botetourt County line. Beginning in Salem at the intersection of Thompson Memorial Drive (Route 311) and North Mill Road, a well-preserved arch and the old roadbed can be seen on the right where North Mill Road crosses Gish Branch. Traces of the old roadbed can be seen at the end of Doyle Street and north of Garst and Locke Streets east of Kessler Mill Road.

A 12-foot masonry arch is located in an open field on the north side of Peters Creek Road (Route 117), just east of its intersection with Cove Road (Route 780). Continuing north on Cove Road towards Salem, the sidewalls of an unfinished 20-foot arch are located just off the south side of the road, opposite the Peters Creek Church of the Brethren.

Immediately west of Carvin Creek, opposite Hollins University and north of Route 11, the old roadbed is evident, including a scattering of large stones intended for use in the bridge over Carvin Creek. These stones were quarried and delivered to the bridge site in 1873 or 1874; some were later salvaged and incorporated in the walls of the Hollins University central heating plant. North of Hollins University, off Route 11 along Route 648, the excavations and embankments forming the old roadbed are now occupied by Birkdale Drive, Old Mill Road, Clifftown Road, and Brown Road. A rectangular masonry culvert is located at the end of Clifftown Road.

The appendix includes detailed maps defining the exact locations of these and other remaining evidences of the Valley Railroad between Lexington and Salem.

The historian's journey is not complete however. Continuing north on Route 11, a historical marker is encountered about four miles north of the small town of Troutville. The marker, titled "The Coming of the Railroad," refers to the Shenandoah Valley Railroad, organized soon after the Civil War. The marker's message reads: "Near here took place the historic meeting of John C. Moomaw and C. M. Thomas that led to the termination of the Shenandoah Valley Railroad at Big Lick (now Roanoke) April 1881. This was the beginning of the City of Roanoke."

This brief message, together with the remaining evidences of the Valley Railroad, serves as the introduction to the story of a 15-year competition to build a railroad through the Valley of Virginia from north of the Potomac River to the Virginia and Tennessee Railroad at Salem. Neither the message nor the traces of the old Valley Railroad do justice to the much larger and complex story of the two competitors, the Valley Railroad and the Shenandoah Valley Railroad, and their sponsors, the Baltimore & Ohio and the Pennsylvania railroads.

In this story abbreviations have been used to designate the principal railroad companies involved. The Valley Railroad is referred to as the VRR, the Shenandoah Valley Railroad as the SVRR, the Atlantic, Mississippi and Ohio as the AM&O, the Baltimore and Ohio as the B&O, the Chesapeake and Ohio as the C&O, and the Norfolk and Western as the N&W.

The founders of the VRR and the SVRR shared a common vision and objective, the construction of a railroad that would assist the communities being served in their recovery from the economic devastation of the Civil War.

The Valley of Virginia had suffered severely in many ways: loss of human life, disruption of families, and destruction or damage to mills, mines, factories, and railroads. Following the war, Virginia and the valley were occupied by Federal troops and governed as a military district. Politically, the citizens had been disenfranchised from national elections; locally they were confronted with the political, social, and economic pressures of the Reconstruction period.

The valley was fortunate that its people were determined to rebuild their lives and communities. Although discouraged, their spirits were not broken, and by early 1866, less than a year after the surrender at Appomattox, their hopes and visions for the future had begun to be evident. Throughout Virginia, community leaders, many of them Confederate veterans, were stepping forward with optimistic plans for rebuilding Virginia's infrastructure and economy. These plans were manifest by numerous charters approved by the General Assembly for railroads, canals, turnpikes, and other public improvements.

It was in this environment that the VRR and the SVRR had their origins.

The two organizing groups were faced with common geographic and economic constraints that would preclude the financial success of two railroads through the Valley of Virginia. Geographically, the valley is relatively narrow, bounded on the east by the Blue Ridge and on the west by the Alleghenies. The valley is separated into two parts on its northern end by Massanutten Mountain. The locations of the two roads were often less than 10 miles apart. In Botetourt County near Troutville, they were adjacent to each other.

The valley's geography also imposed an economic constraint. Each railroad served the same communities, with the exception of the area east of Massanutten Mountain served by the SVRR. Each was in direct competition for the limited local venture capital needed to construct and equip a railroad. Further, the absence of large population centers to generate passenger traffic and the finite agricultural, manufacturing, and mining production within the valley would make it difficult for two railroads to generate sufficient revenue to support operations, retire indebtedness, and provide stockholders a return on their investment.

The two organizing groups did not have the experience or knowledge to foresee the magnitude of the task of creating a railroad. In 1866 and 1867, the organizers of each railroad viewed their separate undertakings as worthy endeavors which would serve and benefit the Valley of Virginia. Each group

Fort Defiance Depot—East of Route 11, Augusta County

Bridge over Middle River—North of Verona, Augusta County

Bridge over Mill Creek, South of Staunton, Opposite Mile Post 219, SB I-81

Lexington Station and Depot, West of Nelson Street (Route 60)

approached its common objective with enthusiasm during a difficult time. The story of their hopes, dreams, visions, and accomplishments, realized and unrealized, is an important part of Virginia's post Civil War history and its railroad heritage.

The organizers of the VRR were drawn from the towns and counties between Staunton and Salem while the SVRR's organizers came from the counties along the lower Shenandoah River; Jefferson County, West Virginia; and Warren and Page Counties in Virginia. Each group's first task was to raise sufficient capital to plan, construct, and equip their proposed railroads. Although each railroad received enthusiastic local support, the financial devastation of the Civil War severely limited the capital resources available locally, and it soon became apparent to the two groups that outside capital was necessary. Each group looked northward and found an interested partner, the B&O Railroad for the VRR and the Pennsylvania Railroad for the SVRR.

Prior to the Civil War, the B&O and the Pennsylvania had been actively pursuing opportunities to expand their systems into the South. They had long viewed the Valley of Virginia as an ideal location for such a railroad. It is part of the Great Valley of the Appalachians, extending from Pennsylvania to Alabama. The Valley of Virginia is a series of lesser valleys separated by low ridges and named for the rivers which drain them. The Shenandoah, the upper James, and the Roanoke Rivers, the eastern waters, drain to the Atlantic Ocean. The New and Holston Rivers, the western waters, drain to the Gulf of Mexico.

For centuries the Great Valley has been an ideal travel way for the movement of animals and humans; first a buffalo path, then an Indian trail, and then a wagon way. It was only natural that it was seen as an ideal and practical route for a railroad connecting the industrial North and the agrarian South. The two Virginia railroads offered the B&O and the Pennsylvania an ideal opportunity to expand their systems into the South.

The period following the Civil War was marked by tremendous growth of the nation's railroad system. During the period from 1865 to 1880, many new railroads were constructed, and smaller existing railroads merged into larger systems. One of the more significant developments during this period was the construction of the Union Pacific and Central Pacific railroads and the connection they formed at Promontory, Utah, on May 10, 1869, creating the nation's first transcontinental rail service.[1] During this period men such as Leland Stanford, Collis P. Huntington, Jay Cooke, Cornelius Vanderbilt, Daniel Drew, Jay Gould, and James Fisk made their marks, both good and bad, on America's post Civil War development. To this list must be added the names of three railroad presidents: John W. Garrett of the B&O, Thomas A. Scott of the Pennsylvania, and William Mahone of the AM&O.

On the Eastern Seaboard, the two major railroads were the B&O and the Pennsylvania. Bitter rivals dating to well before the Civil War, their rivalry intensified following the war and continued into the 1880s.[2] Their rivalry was marked by contentious political battles in Congress and state legislatures for the right to acquire or use existing railroads to extend their systems. The B&O and the Pennsylvania engaged in rate wars that dangerously compromised their financial stability. Even under these circumstances, each continued to expand its system.

The B&O and Pennsylvania systems were generally oriented in an east-west direction; the B&O connected to the port of Baltimore and the Pennsylvania to the port of Philadelphia. Each was expanding westward to various locations on the Ohio River and the Great Lakes, reaching into the Midwest for the opportunity to provide shipping for its agricultural and industrial production. Each railroad was also developing connections into the Northeast and the port of New York. Both were vitally interested in extending their systems into the South, the first step being the completion of one or more railroads across Virginia.

Each railroad had two options for accomplishing this objective. One was to acquire a sufficient number of the existing north-south railroads located east of the Blue Ridge to effect a continuous route across the state. The second option was to construct a new railroad through the Valley of Virginia. Both options were complementary and were pursued concurrently by the B&O and the Pennsylvania. The accompanying map illustrates how each company used these two options in their separate efforts to extend their systems across Virginia into the South.

The second option was of the utmost importance to the officers of the VRR and the

SVRR. For each, it represented the best opportunity to build the railroad needed to revitalize the war-torn Valley of Virginia.

THE NEW RAILROAD OPTION

The northern terminus for a new railroad in the valley was either the B&O main line at Harpers Ferry, West Virginia, on the Potomac River, or the Cumberland Valley Railroad, a branch of the Pennsylvania, at Hagerstown, Maryland. The southern terminus was the Virginia and Tennessee Railroad near Salem. The Virginia and Tennessee had been constructed prior to the Civil War and was independent of either the B&O or the Pennsylvania. Its eastern terminus was Lynchburg where it connected to the Orange and Alexandria and Southside Railroads. Its western terminus was Bristol on the Virginia-Tennessee border, where it connected to the East Tennessee, Virginia and Georgia Railroad, with connections to Knoxville and Chattanooga, Tennessee; Atlanta and Decatur, Georgia; and Memphis, Tennessee, on the Mississippi River.

Construction of a north-south railroad through the Valley of Virginia afforded the B&O and the Pennsylvania an excellent opportunity to extend their systems into the South, provided an agreement to exchange traffic could be negotiated with the Virginia and Tennessee. To exploit this opportunity, the B&O created an alliance with the VRR, and the Pennsylvania developed an agreement with the SVRR soon after they were chartered in 1866 and 1867. However, these alliances would not guarantee success for either the VRR or the SVRR.

Thomas A. Scott

John Work Garrett

William Mahone

Virginia's Railroad Barons

Encyclopedia of American Business History and Biography,
Railroads in the Nineteenth Century

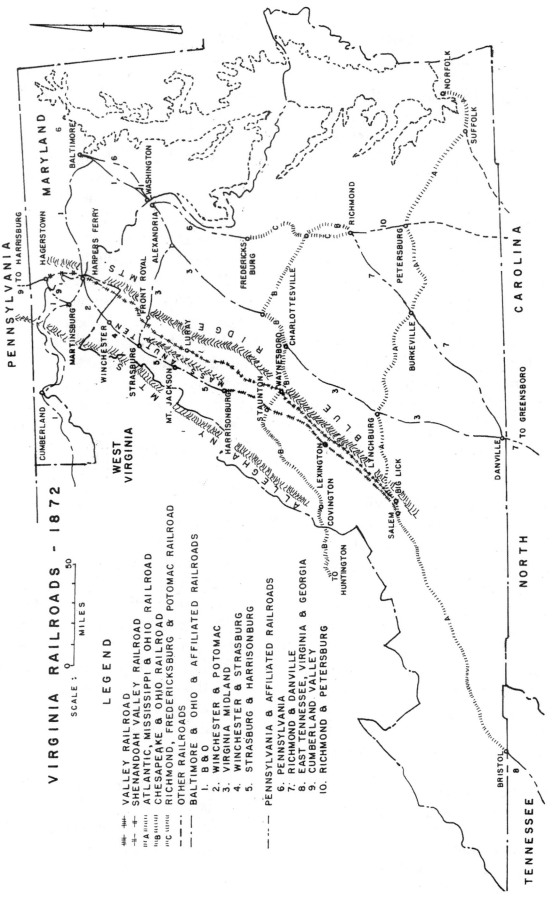

VIRGINIA RAILROADS - 1872

SCALE:
MILES
0   50

LEGEND

VALLEY RAILROAD
SHENANDOAH VALLEY RAILROAD
ATLANTIC, MISSISSIPPI & OHIO RAILROAD
CHESAPEAKE & OHIO RAILROAD
RICHMOND, FREDERICKSBURG & POTOMAC RAILROAD
OTHER RAILROADS
BALTIMORE & OHIO & AFFILIATED RAILROADS

1. B&O
2. WINCHESTER & POTOMAC
3. VIRGINIA MIDLAND
4. WINCHESTER & STRASBURG
5. STRASBURG & HARRISONBURG

PENNSYLVANIA & AFFILIATED RAILROADS

6. PENNSYLVANIA
7. RICHMOND & DANVILLE
8. EAST TENNESSEE, VIRGINIA & GEORGIA
9. CUMBERLAND VALLEY
10. RICHMOND & PETERSBURG

John R. Hildebrand

The extensions of the B&O and Pennsylvania systems into the South were only one of many nationwide expansion projects being considered by the two railroads, and the projects in Virginia were not their first priority. Consequently, the needs and objectives of the local organizing groups and their ability to influence management decisions controlling their destiny were often subverted to the overall interests of the two larger railroads. Thus, the success or failure of the two local railroads became dependent on the ability of the B&O and the Pennsylvania to make the financial commitment necessary to construct a railroad through the Valley of Virginia, while at the same time expanding their systems east of the Blue Ridge and into the Midwest and Northeast.

THE OPTION EAST OF THE BLUE RIDGE

Continuous north-south service through Virginia could also be accomplished by connecting the existing railroads located east of the Blue Ridge. By acquiring and connecting these railroads, the B&O and the Pennsylvania could extend their systems across Virginia. Neither found the task easy, principally because of the influence of one man in the legislative battles created by the Virginia General Assembly's consideration of railroad consolidation acts in 1867, 1870 and 1871. These acts involved divestiture of Virginia's interest in the majority of the railroads in which the state had made substantial investment prior to the Civil War.[3]

These consolidation acts brought to the forefront William Mahone,[4] who was born in Southampton County in December 1826. He was a VMI graduate. Prior to the Civil War, he was president of the Norfolk and Petersburg Railroad. Following distinguished service to the Confederacy, Major General Mahone returned to the presidency of this railroad and rehabilitated its wartime damage. Based on this success, he was named president of the Southside Railroad, connecting Petersburg and Lynchburg, on December 7, 1865. In November 1867, on the recommendation of J. Edgar Thomson, then president of the Pennsylvania, Mahone acquired sufficient interest in the Virginia and Tennessee to be named its president. During this period, Mahone was an influential member of the legislature, a political power throughout Virginia, and a leader in the movement to readjust Virginia's Civil War debts.

Mahone believed that the B&O and Pennsylvania efforts to extend their systems across Virginia would divert the state's east-west rail traffic to the north and the ports of Baltimore and Philadelphia, adversely affecting the economy of eastern Virginia and the port of Norfolk. Mahone, using his influence in the legislature and the news media, opposed the efforts of both railroads to build either a new railroad through the valley or to acquire existing railroads east of the Blue Ridge.

The cornerstone of Mahone's opposition was his plan to consolidate the three railroads he served as president—the Virginia and Tennessee, the Southside, and the Norfolk and Petersburg—by acquiring the state's ownership in each. The plan required legislative approval.

Mahone's first attempt to consolidate the three railroads failed in 1867, but on June 17, 1870, the legislature approved his plan. This allowed Mahone to create the AM&O, a railroad extending four hundred miles from Bristol on the west, through Salem, Lynchburg, and Burkeville to the port of Norfolk on the east.[5] He was then in a position to control the interchange and diversion of east-west traffic to the northern ports and markets served by the B&O and the Pennsylvania. Mahone's AM&O became a major obstacle to the B&O and Pennsylvania plans for north-south railroads across Virginia.

The AM&O later experienced financial difficulties and was placed in receivership in 1876, forcing Mahone to relinquish control. Following his railroad career, Mahone served in the United States Senate from 1881 until 1887. He died in October 1895.

The B&O had recognized the importance of the Virginia and Tennessee to its plans in October 1868 when it attempted to acquire Virginia's majority interest. Here Mahone's opposition to the B&O surfaced. Although his consolidation proposal had been defeated in 1867, he was able to block the 1868 B&O acquisition effort in the legislature, thereby keeping his consolidation plans alive.[6]

The B&O was also active east of the Blue Ridge, creating a connection across Virginia by acquiring the Orange, Alexandria and Manassas Gap[7] and the Lynchburg and Danville Railroads. The B&O's control of these two railroads, renamed the Washington City, Virginia Midland, and Great Southern Railroad, better known as the Virginia Midland, connected the port of Alexandria, Charlottesville, Lynchburg, and Danville. The Virginia Midland had limited value however, because it could not be connected to the B&O system at Washington, D.C.

In 1860, Congress had passed legislation, sponsored by Pennsylvania Railroad interests, preventing the B&O from using the existing railroad bridge across the Potomac River connecting Alexandria and Washington.[8] This required the B&O to ferry its trains across the Potomac River to Alexandria,[9] an inefficient operation. In addition, the opportunity to interchange traffic at Lynchburg was subject to Mahone's control. Finally, the Pennsylvania, through its acquisition of railroads in North Carolina and eastern Tennessee,[10] was in a position to block any plan by the B&O to connect to existing southern railroads at Danville and Bristol.

The Pennsylvania was more successful in its efforts. Following the June 17, 1870, consolidation act creating Mahone's railroad, bills allowing the sale of Virginia's interest in the Richmond and Danville Railroad and other state railroads passed in July 1870 and March 1871 over Mahone's bitter opposition. This legislation allowed the Pennsylvania to acquire the Richmond and Danville Railroad.[11]

Following the acquisition of the Richmond and Danville, the Pennsylvania extended its system from Washington to

Richmond. Through the political influence of its then vice president, Thomas A. Scott, Congress granted the Pennsylvania permission in June 1870 to extend its Baltimore-Washington branch line across the Potomac River railroad bridge to Alexandria.[12] The extension of the Pennsylvania system from Baltimore into Washington had been authorized by Congress in February 1867 and completed in July 1872.[13] These two actions extended the Pennsylvania system into Virginia.

Congressional authorization for the Pennsylvania's use of the Potomac River bridge had been bitterly opposed by John W. Garrett. In 1860, Garrett proposed that the B&O be granted use of the Potomac River bridge, but his plan was defeated through the efforts of Senator Simon Cameron of Pennsylvania, an ally of the Pennsylvania Railroad.[14]

In July 1872, the Pennsylvania also completed an extension from Alexandria to Quantico, where it connected to the Richmond, Fredericksburg and Potomac Railroad.[15] By utilizing this railroad, the Pennsylvania completed the extension of its system from Baltimore into Washington, across the Potomac River, and on across Virginia into North Carolina, where it connected to southern railroads previously acquired by the Pennsylvania. These southern railroads provided connections to Atlanta and the Southeast.

July 1872 marked the successful extension of the Pennsylvania system into the South,[16] an objective accomplished despite the efforts of William Mahone. The extension had the added benefit of preventing the B&O from extending its system south from Danville.

THE BALTIMORE AND OHIO DECISION

With its expansion plans east of the Blue Ridge blocked by the Pennsylvania at Danville, the VRR, extending 113 miles from Harrisonburg to Salem, represented the B&O's last opportunity to extend its system into the South.

For the B&O to implement its southern expansion strategy through sponsorship of the VRR, it was necessary that agreements be negotiated with the AM&O for use of its tracks between Salem and Bristol and with the Pennsylvania to connect to the East Tennessee, Virginia and Georgia at Bristol. Without these agreements, the B&O was prevented from extending its system into the South, just as it had been east of the Blue Ridge. Its only remaining option was to construct an extension of the VRR to existing North Carolina railroads not controlled by the Pennsylvania.

Although past experience with Mahone and Scott gave little reason for optimism, the B&O's officers believed the necessary agreements could be negotiated. Construction of the VRR began in 1872 at Harrisonburg.[17]

THE PENNSYLVANIA RAILROAD DECISION

Thomas A. Scott, mastermind of the Pennsylvania's nationwide expansion efforts in the

1870s, had long visualized the Great Valley of the Appalachians as an ideal route for a railroad into the Southeast. The SVRR, extending 243 miles from Hagerstown to Salem, was an opportunity to complete the first link in such a railroad. The Pennsylvania confirmed its decision to proceed with this plan in March 1870, when a contract for construction of the SVRR was awarded to the Central Improvement Company, a Pennsylvania Railroad subsidiary.

Construction of the SVRR began at the same time Scott was acquiring railroads east of the Blue Ridge. Because these railroads would extend the Pennsylvania system into North Carolina and the Southeast, the SVRR was not as critical to Scott's plans as the VRR was to the B&O's plans. However, the SVRR was more than a connecting link in Scott's overall plan. Located along the western base of the Blue Ridge, it provided the promise of important economic benefits by serving the existing iron ore and mineral deposits along its route.

The final reason for the Pennsylvania's support of the SVRR was its intense and long-standing rivalry with the B&O. The SVRR was a means of compromising and damaging the financial stability of the B&O. While the SVRR's 243-mile length required a much larger investment than the B&O's financial contribution to the 113-mile VRR, the Pennsylvania was prepared to make this financial commitment and to challenge the B&O in the Valley of Virginia.[18]

SETTING THE STAGE

By 1872, both the VRR and the SVRR, supported by the B&O and Pennsylvania Railroads, were under construction. Each had the potential to have farreaching and profound impacts on patterns of growth and economic development in the Shenandoah, upper James and Roanoke Valleys. Nowhere would the success or failure of either or both railroads have a more farreaching impact than in the Roanoke Valley. The following chapters include an analysis of the effect that the completion of the VRR may have had on the growth and development of Salem and Roanoke and a history of the SVRR from its inception until its successful completion to Big Lick. This chapter describes the activities and decisions by Big Lick citizens and SVRR officers which led to the creation of Roanoke. Also included is the history of the VRR which describes the decisions and events leading to its failure.

A history of the effort to build the VRR from Staunton to Salem is also provided. It covers the period from May 1873 until December 1874 and details the work accomplished. Biographical sketches of the engineers, contractors, and workers involved and descriptions and illustrations of the construction methods they used are included.

The appendix is an atlas of maps and photographs of the VRR's location and remains between Lexington and Salem, the 51-mile section which was never completed.

Chapter II
Big Lick Forever?

BACK TO THE FUTURE

The 1881 selection of Big Lick as the connecting point for the SVRR and the N&W changed forever the character and patterns of development and growth throughout the Roanoke Valley. No longer was Salem the county seat, the political and financial center of the Roanoke Valley.

In its place the small community of Big Lick became Roanoke, the Magic City, a growing and thriving railroad, manufacturing, and industrial community. Roanoke became the financial and cultural center of the Roanoke Valley. Salem remained the county seat and a small college town, with diminished political and economic influence.

These changed circumstances created a continuing and friendly rivalry between Salem and Roanoke, with each community extolling its heritage and virtues and, at times, belittling the other's character and traits. This rivalry has spawned many debates suggesting that the development and growth of Roanoke and Salem would have been reversed had the VRR been completed to Salem prior to the arrival of the SVRR at Big Lick.

The answer to such a turn in local history requires an objective analysis of the early histories of the two railroads. The analysis must be based on known facts and conditions, with personal opinions avoided. Dr. E. P. Tompkins of Rockbridge County, in his 1947 "A Sketch of the Valley Railroad," quotes a Staunton attorney who stated: "if the Valley Railroad had been built all the way to Salem, the Shenandoah Valley Railroad would never have been built, and in consequence, the City of Roanoke never would have come into existence." Obviously, this statement does not meet the test of objectivity, but it does pose an intriguing question as to how the futures of Big Lick and Salem might have changed had there been other historical circumstances which prevented the village of Big Lick from becoming the city of Roanoke.

One means of finding an objective answer to this question is to develop and then analyze a series of logical but hypothetical assumptions based on what would have occurred if certain events in the histories of the two railroads had happened differently.

The analysis of such assumptions must be based on how the officers of each company responded to the problems they actually encountered in planning, financing, constructing, and operating their two railroads and the effectiveness of their decisions and solutions.

The early histories of the VRR and the SVRR describe the problems the officers actually encountered and the results of their decisions. Their responses to these actual conditions provide a basis for analyzing the hypothetical events in VRR and SVRR history discussed in the following paragraphs.

The analysis of each of these assumptions led to the conclusions listed at the end of this chapter. It is left to the reader to judge the logic of the writer's assumptions and the validity of his conclusions.

THE CONNECTION OF THE VALLEY AND ATLANTIC, MISSISSIPPI AND OHIO RAILROADS AT SALEM

Completion of the VRR to Salem with a connection to the AM&O would not have guaranteed Salem the growth and development later experienced by Roanoke. For Salem to have developed as the Roanoke Valley's leading manufacturing, industrial, and railroad center, it was necessary that the VRR and its sponsor, the B&O, develop sufficient traffic at Salem to generate the

levels of income which would require and support a substantial infrastructure of yards, shops, and offices.

The opportunity to develop such levels of revenue-producing traffic was extremely limited. Because of William Mahone's opposition to the B&O's efforts to extend its system into Virginia, there was no reason to believe that he would have agreed to permit any diversion of AM&O traffic which would benefit the VRR and the B&O.

The VRR's economic potential at Salem was therefore limited to the traffic generated locally in Roanoke and surrounding counties. This situation would have been avoided had the B&O been successful in its effort to purchase the Virginia and Tennessee in 1868. This effort had failed however, because of Mahone's opposition in the Virginia General Assembly. The failure to acquire this railroad eliminated the opportunity for the VRR and the B&O to benefit from the traffic generated later when branch lines were extended into the coal fields of southwestern Virginia and West Virginia.

Without B&O control of the Virginia and Tennessee, Salem would have been the southern limit of the B&O system. There would have been no requirement for general offices, hotels, machine shops for manufacturing locomotives and cars, yards and other railroad infrastructure which played such a significant role in the growth and development of Roanoke. On the B&O system, this infrastructure was located at Baltimore and did not need to be duplicated. The maximum development which could have been anticipated at Salem would have been a passenger station and freight depot, a means to reverse train operations and facilities to hold livestock and store agricultural products.

With the VRR requiring a limited infrastructure and lacking access to the markets served by the AM&O, Salem would not have received the economic benefits needed to develop beyond its present size. Further, the railroad's location through Salem would have hindered the later development of the residential areas north of Main Street and the Roanoke College campus. The VRR's economic benefits to Salem would have been minimal when compared to the economic benefits later provided by the SVRR at Big Lick.

SOUTH FROM WAYNESBORO

Completion of the VRR to Salem would not have deterred the development of the SVRR. The SVRR's principal objective was to provide rail service to the West Virginia and Virginia communities located along the lower Shenandoah River and to develop the mineral resources along the western slopes of the Blue Ridge.

For its sponsors, the construction of the SVRR was critical to their individual business interests, to the economies of the communities along its route and to the development of the area's natural resources. The Shenandoah Iron Works, owned by William Milnes, Jr., was a typical example. Located between Luray and Waynesboro, it manufactured pig iron processed from local deposits of iron ore. This product was of limited value without a convenient railroad to deliver it

to the Pennsylvania mills. The SVRR, because of its location, was the only railroad able to provide this service. There was no reason for it to abandon its plans, even had the VRR been completed to Salem.

The SVRR accomplished its principal objective when it completed construction to the C&O at Waynesboro. The needs and requirements of its sponsors had been met and there was no compelling reason to extend the railroad any farther south. The SVRR's sponsors had recognized this circumstance in 1872, when they eliminated the work south of Waynesboro from the Central Improvement Company contract.

Without the occurrence of some significant event requiring the extension of the SVRR to Big Lick, Waynesboro would have become the southern terminus of the SVRR, and Big Lick would have remained a small Roanoke County community.

THE ROAD TAKEN

This significant event occurred on February 10, 1881, when E. W. Clark and Company acquired the Atlantic, Mississippi and Ohio and reorganized it as the Norfolk and Western Railroad. To develop the full potential of its acquisition, the Clark company required a connection into the industrial North. This was readily accomplished by extending the SVRR south from Waynesboro.

CONCLUSIONS

Once the need to extend the SVRR to a connection with the N&W had been established, the creation of Roanoke was assured. There is no historical basis to support Dr. Tompkins' assumption that completion of the VRR into Salem would have eliminated the need to build the SVRR to Big Lick, with the result that Roanoke would not have come into existence. The Shenandoah Valley Railroad succeeded for numerous reasons, including:

- Stronger local leadership. Beginning with William Milnes, Jr's. election as a director in 1870, he provided the leadership needed to keep the SVRR from failing during a difficult economic period. He was not discouraged by the suspension of construction in 1874. Instead, he negotiated traffic agreements that were critical to the SVRR's ultimate success. From 1876 to 1878, he continually sought a means of financing and completing construction. Milnes, because of his imaginative and tenacious leadership, his standing in the local communities, his political service in Congress, his understanding of the importance of railroads to economic development, his contacts in the Philadelphia financial community, and his personal investment, must be recognized as one of the people responsible for the ultimate completion of the Shenandoah Valley Railroad.

  The only Valley leader with comparable abilities was Michael G. Harman. Following Harman's death in December 1877, there was an unfilled void in the VRR's local leadership, resulting in the local communities losing influence in the management of the company.

- Stronger financial backing. Following the Panic of 1873, neither the Pennsylvania nor the B&O was in position to financially support or generate the additional capital required to complete the two railroads. The SVRR was fortunate that the Pennsylvania relinquished its control and E. W. Clark and Company became interested in its development. This company's expertise and experience in financing and constructing railroads provided the SVRR a resource never available to the VRR.

- Stronger and more competent management. The leadership and management abilities of Frederick J. Kimball were critical. Without his abilities in railroad construction and operations, the building of the SVRR could have floundered. Without his insight into the economic potential of the coal deposits of southwestern Virginia and West Virginia, the Clark company might not have purchased the AM&O. Robert Garrett and the B&O vice presidents who followed him were primarily interested in the business affairs of the B&O. Kimball had no such distraction. His sole objective was to build the SVRR. His abilities were based on a lifetime of experience and thorough knowledge of all facets of the railroad industry. The B&O was unable to provide anyone of like ability until Samuel Spencer was named president of the VRR in 1881, too late to influence decisions that might have resulted in its completion.

- The creation of the N&W Railroad. E. W. Clark and Company's acquisition of the AM&O ensured the SVRR's extension from Waynesboro into the Roanoke Valley. When the B&O failed to acquire the Virginia and Tennessee Railroad in 1868, the opportunity for the VRR to benefit from the coal traffic from southwestern Virginia and West Virginia was lost.

- The family relationship of Milnes and Kimball, his nephew, that was instrumental in interesting the Clark company in the potential of the SVRR.

THE KIND HAND OF FATE

The histories of the SVRR and VRR which follow support these conclusions. Even so, the intervention of the kind hand of fate was necessary to ensure the creation of Roanoke.

There were two events in 1876 and 1881 that could have altered the course of events leading to the completion of the SVRR to Big Lick. Had either event taken a different direction, Roanoke would not have come into being. That this did not occur can only be attributed to the same kind hand of fate which produced the Milnes-Kimball family relationship.

The first occurred in 1876, when the SVRR's temporary lease of the VRR was canceled, preventing it from exercising its option to complete the VRR's unfinished construction between Staunton and Salem. Had this lease remained in effect, the SVRR's connection at Big Lick would not have been needed.

The second event was John C. Moomaw's 1881 suggestion to the leaders of the Big Lick community that they make a monetary contribution to the SVRR for the purchase of right-of-way into Big Lick. Without his suggestion, Bonsack could have become the Magic City, and Big Lick would have forever remained a small community.

Chapter III
A History of the Shenandoah Valley Railroad, 1867–1882

1867–1870

The organizers of the Shenandoah Valley Railroad planned to build a railroad from Hagerstown, Maryland, to Salem, Virginia. At Hagerstown it would connect to the Cumberland Valley Railroad, a branch of the Pennsylvania Railroad providing connections to the Pennsylvania system at Harrisburg, Pennsylvania. At Salem, it would connect to the Virginia and Tennessee Railroad, an independent operation. There were no existing railroads along its proposed route, and 243 miles of new construction was required. This was over twice the 113 miles of new construction required by the Valley Railroad, which was able to use three existing railroads between Harrisonburg and its northern connection to the B&O mainline at Harpers Ferry, West Virginia.

With the SVRR located in Maryland, West Virginia, and Virginia, three separate legislative authorizations were required to obtain a charter. This took more than three years, delaying the planning and organizing of the company until 1870, four years after the VRR's 1866 organizing convention.

The Virginia General Assembly was the first to act when it passed charter legislation on February 2, 1867.[1] The act provided that the charter would become effective when $200,000 of the $4,000,000 authorized capital had been subscribed in stock at $100 per share. The road's Virginia section was to begin at Harpers Ferry or some other point on the Potomac River, proceed south through the counties of Warren and Page, at or near Port Republic in Rockingham County, continue south through the counties of Augusta, Rockbridge, and Botetourt, and connect to the Virginia and Tennessee Railroad at or near Salem in Roanoke County. Branch lines were to be provided from suitable points on the main line to Harrisonburg in Rockingham County, to Gordonsville in Orange County, routed through Stanardsville in Greene County and to Lexington in Rockbridge County. The charter did not require depots at specific locations or calendar limitations in completing the work before other railroads became operational. Three commissioners were named at each of eleven locations along the route to receive stock subscriptions.

The Virginia charter was amended April 2, 1870, to allow construction of branch or lateral lines not exceeding 10 miles, to connect to mines, lands, works, or factories owned or operated by the SVRR.[2] The significance of this legislation became apparent in 1881 during the construction of the railroad south from Waynesboro.

On February 25, 1870, the West Virginia legislature granted the company a charter to construct the railroad through Jefferson County from Charles Town to a crossing of the Potomac River at Shepherdstown. On April 4, 1870, the Maryland legislature granted a charter to extend the railroad from the Potomac River, at any point between Harpers Ferry and Williamsport, Pennsylvania, at or near Shepherdstown, extending to Hagerstown.[3]

The company's Virginia charter was amended again on July 8, 1870, allowing construction of a branch line from the vicinity of Salem to Danville, Virginia.[4]

With the enactment of the charter legislation in the three states completed, the SVRR's sponsors were ready to organize and begin planning the construction and financing of the railroad. On March 14, 1870, in Luray, Peter B. Borst, a Luray attorney, was elected the company's first president. Borst was born in New York about 1827. He served as Page County delegate to the 1861 secession

convention in Richmond and later served as Page County's Commonwealth attorney.[5] The board of directors elected at this meeting included Mann Spittler, Thomas M. Almond, and William Milnes, Jr. of Page County; three men from Philadelphia, William Painter, B. K. Jamison, and George H. Bardwell; and one from New York, J. A. Walker. Other directors were William H. Travers from Jefferson County and Samuel Hoar of Rockbridge County.[6]

On July 21, 1870, the Central Improvement Company was awarded a contract to build the railroad from Shepherdstown to Salem for $35,000 a mile.[7] The approximate distance was 224 miles, making the total value of the contract about $7,800,000. Central Improvement, a subsidiary of the Pennsylvania Railroad,[8] was to be paid in first mortgage bonds at 70 cents on the dollar, in second mortgage bonds at 50 cents on the dollar, in county bonds to the extent subscribed at 70 cents on the dollar, with the balance to be paid in the stock of the company at cash market value at completion of the work.[9] The Central Improvement contract determined that the Pennsylvania Railroad would play a major role in building the SVRR.

The terms of the construction contract provide an insight into the SVRR's $4,000,000 capitalization. Capital available from private investors was limited, as were financial contributions from the communities being served. Only Page and Clarke Counties in Virginia and Jefferson County and Shepherdstown in West Virginia elected to participate. Page County subscribed $200,000, Clarke County $100,000, and Jefferson County $250,000.[10] County bonds were used to purchase right-of-way in the participating county. Shepherdstown subscribed $8,000, contingent on shops and maintenance facilities being built there.[11] None of the counties south of Page County named in the charter purchased SVRR stock. Private investment was slightly more than $100,000.

The major source of capital was derived from the sale of mortgage bonds, guaranteed by the Pennsylvania Railroad. Even with this support and without tangible assets, the SVRR was a risky investment from its beginning.

1871

The influence of the Pennsylvania Railroad was confirmed at the April 18 stockholders' meeting in Charles Town, when Thomas A. Scott, then a Pennsylvania vice president, was elected the SVRR's second president, replacing Peter B. Borst.[12]

Thomas A. Scott was born December 23, 1823, at London, Franklin County, Pennsylvania. He began his career with the Pennsylvania Railroad in 1850 as station agent at Hollidaysburg, Pennsylvania. Scott advanced rapidly: he was named Pittsburgh agent in 1851; third assistant superintendent, western division, in 1852; general superintendent of the western division in 1853; vice president in 1860; and president in 1874. He was considered one of the "most important railroad officials" in the United States during the 19th century. During the Civil War, he was commissioned a colonel by President Abraham Lincoln and served as assistant secretary of war in 1861 and 1862.[13]

Scott was an ideal choice for the SVRR's presidency. He was familiar with Virginia politics. Beginning in 1870, he led the Pennsylvania's successful effort to expand its system through Virginia into the South by acquiring several existing Virginia railroads.[14] In the course of this effort, Scott was accused of giving Governor Gilbert C. Walker's brother shares of Pennsylvania Railroad stock for his services,[15] illustrating the bitter level of opposition by the B&O and William Mahone to his acquisitions. Mahone's opposition was particularly virulent, referring at one point to Scott's efforts as "infernal designs."[16]

Scott, through the Southern Security Company, a holding company in which the Pennsylvania participated, also acquired 13 different Southern railroads, extending the Pennsylvania system some two thousand miles into North and South Carolina, Tennessee, Georgia, Alabama, and Mississippi.[17]

Scott also played a leading role in other railroad expansion activities. He was involved with the Northern Pacific Railroad and was named president of the Union Pacific Railroad in 1871 when it was acquired by the Pennsylvania. The Union Pacific venture proved unsuccessful, but Scott continued to seek a means of extending the Pennsylvania to the Pacific Ocean. In 1872, he was named president of the Texas and Pacific Railroad, extending from Vicksburg, Mississippi, to San Diego, California.[18] Given the national scope of these plans, Scott and the Pennsylvania would find it difficult to invest sufficient time and energy to develop and include the 243-mile SVRR in their larger plan to create southern trunk routes and a transcontinental railroad.

1871 was also the beginning of a long period of dissatisfaction with the progress of the Central Improvement Company. The company had concluded that its 1870 construction bid was not sufficient to cover the actual cost of construction. In August, the SVRR's directors received a proposal from the company to terminate the contract for the amount already paid, plus costs incurred. The offer was declined.[19]

1872

Scott was re-elected to a second term as president at the annual stockholders' meeting on April 9 at Front Royal. He was also serving as president of the Texas and Pacific. William Milnes, Jr. was among the directors re-elected. One of the new directors was Upton L. Boyce of Clarke County.[20] Boyce's election proved critical to the railroad's ultimate success as he later assumed an increasing level of responsibility in the company's financial affairs and construction activities.

Problems with Central Improvement continued. By June, the bridge over the Shenandoah River north of Front Royal had not been started. The construction company was requested to begin work on the bridge as early as practical, to make arrangements

for its early completion, and to report on its progress at the next directors' meeting.[21]

The requested progress report was not received at the July 25 meeting. However, the Central Improvement contract was modified to extend the completion date from August 1872 to January 1, 1875, and to delete the work between the C&O Railroad in Augusta County and the Virginia and Tennessee in Roanoke County,[22] which by August 1872 had been incorporated into William Mahone's AM&O. By deleting the work south of the C&O, the length of the contract was reduced 94 miles for a savings of almost $3,300,000. The method of payment was not changed. The Pennsylvania provided financial support with a $3,500,000 loan guaranteeing the SVRR's mortgage bonds.[23]

The directors were undaunted by the lack of progress. In early September, the Cumberland Valley Railroad was asked to aid in the construction of the section from Shepherdstown to Hagerstown.[24]

1873

At the annual stockholders' meeting in Philadelphia on May 21, President Scott outlined the need to construct the SVRR as "rapidly as the stringent condition of the money market would allow" in order to take advantage of a connection with the C&O in Augusta County. The extension of the C&O from Covington to Huntington, West Virginia, had been completed on January 29, creating a 428-mile railroad connecting Richmond and Huntington on the Ohio River. During its construction, vast coal deposits were discovered along its route in West Virginia.[25] Scott viewed these coal deposits, together with the development of iron ore and other minerals located along the SVRR's route, as offering the potential for the manufacture of iron products on the scale then existing in the Lehigh Valley of Pennsylvania.

Scott's report included other items. One was a request from Staunton for a direct connection to that city. The request included the promise of right-of-way, financial aid and community support, but would have required a modification of the location south of Page County. A committee was formed to meet with Staunton's representatives and determine what could be accomplished and its estimated cost. Although an arrangement was never negotiated, it received serious consideration. The Staunton request may have been an indication of its dissatisfaction with the progress and activities of the VRR-B&O partnership.

A second item was the advice to delay establishing the route north of Shepherdstown until the location of railroads being constructed in Maryland and Pennsylvania were established. These roads offered better connections to Philadelphia and New York, but if they failed to develop, the connection at Hagerstown remained a viable solution.

A third item outlined the progress accomplished by Central Improvement. Work had been severely affected by winter conditions, and the January 1, 1875, completion date would be delayed. Gradation and masonry

from Shepherdstown to Front Royal was almost finished and would be completed by June 15. The work on the 17 miles from Front Royal to Luray had begun with completion scheduled for November 1. The work south of Luray to the C&O would not begin until a location was established.

Finally, negotiations were underway with the Pennsylvania and Cumberland Valley for marketing the SVRR's first mortgage bonds. Both companies believed the SVRR and its traffic potential was a sound investment which would result in a fair price for its bonds.[26]

A May 1, 1873, Memorandum of Agreement for a traffic agreement with the Pennsylvania and the Cumberland Valley was accepted by the directors. This agreement was never ratified and negotiations with the two companies continued for many years.[27] The directors also authorized similar contracts with the Penn Central, C&O, and Philadelphia and Reading railroads.[28]

Scott resigned the SVRR presidency on June 17, less than 30 days after the May 21 stockholders' meeting, giving as his reason the press of other activities with the Pennsylvania and Union Pacific. Thomas B. Kennedy of Chambersburg, Pennsylvania, a Cumberland Valley vice president, was named the company's third president.[29] On July 15, he declined the office because of his health. Kennedy had other reasons for he was named president of the Cumberland Valley in October, a position he held until 1905. William M. McLellan of Chambersburg was then named the company's fourth president.[30]

Being from Chambersburg, the Cumberland Valley's headquarters, McLellan was likely an officer of that railroad. This was the board's last action of 1873.

An important event that occurred during the year was the Virginia General Assembly's passage of legislation allowing five or more people to form a joint stock company, excluding turnpikes, railroads, canals, and banks.[31] The significance of this legislation became apparent in 1881, when the Roanoke Machine Works were organized.

Another event with greater impact occurred in September, when the nation experienced the beginning of a economic depression which would last until 1877. The depression was caused by the failure of the Jay Cooke banking company, the agent selling the bonds used to finance the construction of the Northern Pacific Railroad. The Cooke company had invested heavily in the railroad company, and when the sale of the Northern Pacific bonds failed to provide sufficient funds to complete its construction, Cooke's bank was unable to cover the deficit. On September 19, the Cooke company closed its offices, leading to a nationwide collapse and loss of confidence in the entire banking system and a withdrawal of investments in railroad projects.[32]

1874

1874 was a turbulent year for the SVRR and the Pennsylvania. On May 27, the Pennsylvania's president, J. Edgar Thomson, died and was succeeded by Scott. Thomson's

death was attributed to financial pressures resulting from the Panic of 1873 and an inquiry by Pennsylvania stockholders into the company's many expansion projects. The stockholders were particularly critical of the participation in the Southern Security Company.

Beginning in 1870, Thomson and Scott had involved the Pennsylvania in numerous expansion projects, two of which, the Union Pacific and the Texas and Pacific Railroads, included investment of their personal financial assets. Scott provided the leadership for these projects, including the involvement with the Southern Security Company.

The 13 Southern railroads controlled by Southern Security in 1872 included the Richmond and Danville and the Richmond and Petersburg Railroads. Following the 1873 Panic, five of the larger roads in this group saw their earnings decline over 20 percent. As a result, the Pennsylvania charged off its entire investment in all the companies except the Richmond and Danville. When Scott assumed the Pennsylvania presidency, he was confronted with restoring its financial health. He accomplished this by reducing system mileage and selling unprofitable lines, a first step in the ultimate dissolution of the Pennsylvania-SVRR relationship.[33]

The SVRR had its own problems. In March, President McLellan and Directors Milnes and Boyce met with Central Improvement to determine if the company was capable of completing its contract.[34] The three officers concluded that the company was not capable and, on April 7, Central Improvement's president was informed that unless work resumed immediately the contract would be canceled.[35]

Central Improvement was unable to resume work, and on December 23 the directors named a committee to arrange an equitable settlement for completed work. The committee was also authorized to confer with individuals and corporations to arrange financing and construction contracts for completing the railroad.

Negotiations to develop a traffic contract with the Cumberland Valley continued. A modification requiring the SVRR to construct the Shepherdstown-Hagerstown section was proposed. The SVRR agreed, contingent upon its bonds yielding sufficient funds for the construction.[36]

Another result of the 1873 Panic which ultimately affected the SVRR occurred in January when Mahone's AM&O was unable to pay the interest on its bonds.[37]

1875

Activities during 1875 included the traffic contract negotiations, a search for a means of resuming construction, and the election of William Milnes, Jr. as vice president at the April 6 directors' meeting. At this meeting, President McLellan and Milnes were instructed to have the pending traffic contracts with the Pennsylvania, Cumberland Valley, and other railroads executed.[38]

In May, U. L. Boyce was named to act with McLellan and Milnes. McLellan was authorized to arrange and execute construction contracts which would result in early completion of the road.[39]

1876

1876 was an eventful year. At a directors' meeting in Charles Town, President McLellan advised that revisions to the May 1, 1873, traffic agreement with the Pennsylvania and Cumberland Valley were necessary. The revised agreement, dated February 3, 1876, cancelled the May 1 agreement. It was signed by Thomas A. Scott for the Pennsylvania, by Thomas B. Kennedy for the Cumberland Valley, and by William McLellan for the SVRR.[40]

At the April 4 stockholders' meeting, William Milnes, Jr. was elected the company's fifth president,[41] replacing William McLellan. His election was the beginning of a shift away from the influence of the Pennsylvania and the Cumberland Valley Railroads to Philadelphia banking interests.

Milnes was born in Lancashire, England, in 1828 and immigrated to Pennsylvania about 1855. He was an industrialist and moved to Page County following the Civil War. There he purchased the Shenandoah Iron Works which manufactured pig iron. It was through his interest in developing the mineral resources of Page County and the Shenandoah Valley that he became one of the first directors of the railroad and one of its largest private stockholders. Milnes was elected to Congress in 1869 as a Conservative, and took his seat in the 41st Congress

William Milnes, Jr.
1828–1891
Special Collections Department,
University Libraries of Virginia Tech

in January 1870. This Congress was the first since 1865 in which Virginians who had not participated in the 1861 Secession Convention were eligible to serve. Milnes had not participated in this convention and was eligible to stand for election. Milnes and his wife, Elizabeth Johns, had six children. Milnes died in 1891 and was buried in Shenandoah, a town originally named Milnes.[42]

Following Milnes' election, the directors elected U. L. Boyce vice president.[43] Upton Lawerence Boyce, an attorney and farmer, was born in Kentucky in 1831. Prior to the

Civil War, he practiced law in St. Louis, Missouri, and moved to Clarke County in 1868 where he continued to practice law with his partner, Uriel S. Wright, with offices in Winchester and Berryville. Boyce served in the Union cavalry during the Civil War, attaining the rank of colonel. He was an influential citizen of Clarke County and instrumental in the passage of the county's $100,000 stock subscription to the SVRR. He was active in the railroad's development. Beginning with his election to the board of directors in 1874, he served on many committees, particularly those involved in negotiating leases, right-of-way purchases, traffic agreements, construction contracts, and financing.

As a director and vice president, Boyce was intimately involved with officials of the Pennsylvania. Thomas A. Scott supposedly offered Boyce $50,000 if he could make the SVRR a success. When the railroad was completed to Big Lick in June 1882, Boyce reminded Scott of his offer and reportedly received his check for $50,000. The problem with this story is that Scott died on May 21, 1882, before the railroad was completed. There is no question, however, of the importance of Boyce's leadership. After Milnes and Frederick J. Kimball, he had the greatest influence on the ultimate success of the SVRR. The town of Boyce, Clarke County, located on the railroad two miles north of US Highway 17, was named for him.[44]

At the April 10 directors' meeting, the execution of traffic contracts with the Pennsylvania and Cumberland Valley were authorized. The need for this authorization is unclear since an agreement with the two railroads had been signed on February 3. Further negotiations over finer points in the contract may have been necessary. The execution of traffic agreements with the Western Maryland, Philadelphia and Reading, and Lehigh Valley Railroads were also authorized, provided that terms similar to the Pennsylvania and Cumberland Valley contracts were included.

The directors instructed Milnes and Boyce to make a financial settlement with Central Improvement and the Pennsylvania, arrange a contract for completion of construction, and arrange for the sale of first mortgage bonds. Finally, Milnes was to appoint a committee to arrange for construction financing.[45]

Earlier in 1876, Milnes had initiated negotiations to lease the completed and operating section of the VRR between Harrisonburg and Staunton. This was a practical means of making connection to Staunton and the C&O requested by Staunton interests in 1873. On July 19, Milnes reported that a temporary 15-year lease had been negotiated for the 26-mile Harrisonburg-Staunton section, with the understanding that the lease could be extended to any desired length south of Staunton. The directors ratified the lease and Milnes proceeded to procure the staff, motive power and rolling stock necessary for operations.

At this same meeting, the directors reaffirmed their previous action to "perfect any arrangement deemed best for the company to purchase, lease, operate or make other arrangement for using line or lines of other railroads as if the same had been specifically authorized by the stockholders." Milnes and Boyce were also instructed to finalize settlements with Central Improvement and the company's other creditors on terms they considered in the company's best interest.[46]

The first in a series of events which would ultimately lead to the extension of the SVRR into the Roanoke Valley occurred on June 6, when the AM&O was placed in receivership. Henry Fink, its general superintendent, who later played a significant role in the development of the Norfolk and Western Railroad as its third president,[47] was one of the receivers.

1877

Although construction did not resume in 1877, Milnes and the officers were occupied with numerous planning and administrative activities. In January, Boyce was named to receive the payments for carrying mail on the leased section of the VRR. In February, a proposal by Berkeley County, West Virginia, to subscribe $75,000 for an extension through the county from Charles Town to Martinsburg[48] was considered.

Milnes was re-elected president at the April 2 stockholders' meeting. He reported that the VRR had refused to honor its 1876 lease of the section south of Staunton, eliminating the opportunity for the SVRR to utilize the partially completed VRR construction between Staunton and Salem.

Had Milnes been able to combine the 113-mile VRR with the partially completed work on the SVRR between Shepherdstown and

Luray, only two segments between Shepherdstown and Salem would have remained on which no work had been accomplished: one, the 16-mile section between Hagerstown and Shepherdstown; the second, a 37-mile connection between Luray and Harrisonburg, routed through either Elkton or Port Republic, a total of 53 miles of new construction. This compared to 144 miles of new construction along the route from Luray through Waynesboro to a connection near Salem. This would have reduced construction and right-of-way costs significantly.

With the failure to consummate the agreement, the VRR was given a six-month termination notice. The Harrisonburg-Staunton section was returned to the VRR, rolling stock was withdrawn, the agents paid off, and all other liabilities satisfied.[49]

On the positive side, Milnes believed that construction could be resumed in 1877 and it was imperative that arrangements be made to connect the SVRR to an operating railroad. To accomplish this, the $75,000 subscription from Berkeley County to construct a branch line from Charles Town to a connection to the Cumberland Valley at Martinsburg was accepted. The money was to be spent in Berkeley County. The original plan to construct the main line into Shepherdstown, as required by the Jefferson County stock subscription, was retained.[50] The Martinsburg branch allowed the SVRR the option of eliminating the Shepherdstown to Hagerstown segment.

On August 9 Milnes was authorized to select an engineer to establish the route of the Charles Town-Martinsburg branch line and to request the aid of Berkeley and Jefferson Counties in securing right-of-way.[51]

1878

In March, negotiations began with the John Satterlee Company and Alfred Creveling of New York City to resume construction and provide operating equipment.[52] John Satterlee was a successful railroad contractor with ties to the Philadelphia banking community.[53]

The Satterlee contract provided for two branches at the northern end of the line. One branch would begin at Martinsburg, the other at Shepherdstown. They would connect at a point within three miles of Charles Town and then run south to the C&O in the vicinity of Waynesboro, a total distance of 153 miles. The contract was signed on April 3 and presented to the board of directors at a special meeting held in Winchester on April 27. The contract, with amendments, was approved.[54]

Milnes was re-elected at the annual stockholders' meeting on May 1, but only after two other nominations failed. Eleven directors were named. U. L. Boyce was re-elected vice president, and B. K. Jamison of Philadelphia, one of the original directors, was named treasurer.

Milnes reported that construction was proceeding and attributed the five-year suspension of work to the "continued and increased stringency of the money market in the country." He advised that construction had resumed only because the company's creditors had postponed their liens on the first mortgage bonds. In response, the officers and directors agreed to serve without compensation during the coming year.[55]

With the award of a construction contract, arrangements for financing construction and purchasing equipment were initiated. In December, the directors, acting in accordance with authority granted by the stockholders in June 1871 and September 1872, reduced the amount of authorized bonds to $2,250,000, or $15,000 per mile.

The bonds were secured by a first mortgage on the company's branches, main line, real estate, and franchises, with the Farmers Loan and Trust Company of New York serving as trustee. The mortgage was dated January 1, 1879, and ran for 30 years. The bonds paid seven percent interest annually, with principal and interest paid in gold.[56]

1879

1879 was the pivotal year in the SVRR's history. In early January, a committee was appointed to prepare plans for building shops and depots.[57] At the May stockholders' meeting in Winchester, Milnes, Boyce, and Jamison were re-elected to their offices. Eleven directors were named, and John Satterlee was appointed superintendent.

Milnes advised the stockholders that construction had started at Duffields Depot on the B&O and 20 miles of railroad in good running order had been completed between Shepherdstown and the Jefferson County-Clarke County line at the West Virginia-Virginia border.[58] Concurrently, Satterlee was working on the roadbed between the Jefferson County-Clarke County line and Riverton on the Shenandoah River north of Front Royal. This roadbed had been graded by Central Improvement in 1872 and early 1873.

The design at Duffields Depot was modified to eliminate the at-grade crossing with the B&O by providing trestle-work and a bridge. This separated the two railroads, precluding any interchange of traffic with the B&O and diversion of Shenandoah Valley trade to the port of Baltimore.

Surveys indicated that the best outlet for the 20 miles of completed and operating railroad was a 9.5-mile branch line to Beddington Station. This station was located north of Martinsburg on the Martinsburg and Potomac Railroad, a road controlled and managed by the Cumberland Valley.[59] It provided connections to the Pennsylvania and other railroads at Harrisburg. Construction would be financed with first mortgage bonds, provided the $2,250,000 total issue for the entire road was not exceeded.

Other stockholder actions included an invitation to Winchester to extend a line from that city to Berryville and an authorization to issue second mortgage bonds for its construction. Proceedings against stockholders delinquent in paying their stock subscriptions were also authorized.[60]

On June 20, the Satterlee Company sold its construction and equipment contract to the Shenandoah Valley Construction Company, a firm organized and owned by E. W. Clark and Company, a Philadelphia banking firm specializing in railroad development and investments.[61] The Clark company's purchase of the Satterlee contract committed its financial and management resources to the SVRR and marked the end of the Pennsylvania's support of the SVRR. While Scott and Central Improvement continued to hold stock, their participation was no longer significant.

On July 15, the SVRR advised Shenandoah Valley Construction that its acquisition of the Satterlee contract was acceptable. However, the SVRR had not reserved sufficient funds to meet its liabilities or to operate the road, and it requested that $1,000 a mile of first mortgage bonds be reserved for these expenses.

On July 24, Shenandoah Valley Construction agreed to change the contract and proposed that it receive $300,000 of capital stock upon acceptance of the proposal, $13,000 a mile of first mortgage bonds, and $5,500 a mile of stock as work was completed. Upon completion of the road to the C&O, it would receive an additional $200,000 of capital stock.

The proposal also included the following conditions:

- The branch line from Shepherdstown would be built and the Martinsburg branch eliminated.

- Locomotives, cars, and other rolling stock would not be provided as specified in the Satterlee contract.

- County bonds were preferred for payment of completed work. For the work in Page County, payments were to be made in that county's bonds, if available. The railroad company was admonished to avoid delays in obtaining county bonds.

- The railroad company would retain $2,000 per mile of first mortgage bonds for the purchase of right-of-way and payment of its other liabilities.

- Shenandoah Valley Construction would not be liable for claims against the work accomplished by the Satterlee Company or against the 5,000 shares of railroad company stock it had purchased from Satterlee.

The proposal was accepted on July 24 and made a part of the construction contract.[62] While its terms were not as favorable as those in the Satterlee contract, the active involvement of the Clark company in the financing, construction, and management of the SVRR proved invaluable.

The involvement of the Clark company brought to center stage Frederick J. Kimball. He would play a significant role in the timely completion of the SVRR to Waynesboro, the Clark company's acquisition of the AM&O, its reorganization as the Norfolk and Western Railroad and the construction of a major railroad operations center with facilities to manufacture the company's motive power and rolling stock. Kimball's foresight, financial contacts, engineering abilities, and leadership proved indispensable to the completion of the SVRR and its incorporation into the N&W system.

E. W. Clark and Company's interest in the SVRR had its origins in the family relationship of Milnes and his nephew, Frederick J. Kimball, and their shared interest in developing a successful business venture. Milnes needed a more efficient means of shipping the products manufactured by his Shenandoah Iron Works. He had been using horse-drawn wagons and river flatboats to reach the nearest railroad, a costly, inconvenient, and inefficient operation. The SVRR was an ideal solution which would also serve other industries located along the Shenandoah River.[63]

Frederick J. Kimball
1844–1903
Special Collections Department,
University Libraries of Virginia Tech

Kimball, a partner in the Clark company,[64] had advised Milnes of its financial resources and interest in developing railroads. Kimball also viewed the SVRR as an opportunity for personal financial gain. As president of Clark's railroad construction company, he could provide the direction and leadership necessary to complete, equip, manage, and operate the railroad.

Kimball was first and foremost a railroader. He was born in Philadelphia in 1844 and began his railroad career at age 18 when he was employed by the Pennsylvania Railroad as a survey party rodman. Two years later, he was promoted to engineer of shops. Lacking a formal education, Kimball went to England in 1868 to work in the railroad shops, gaining experience in a more advanced railroad industry than existed in the United States. Kimball returned to this country after two years and joined E. W. Clark and Company in 1870 as a partner. In 1878, the Clark company named him president of the Shenandoah Valley Construction Company. Kimball was named president of the SVRR in 1881 and N&W president in 1883. Kimball died in 1903.[65]

E. W. Clark and Company was founded in 1837 as a private bank. The founder, Enoch W. Clark, died in 1857 and was succeeded by Edward W. Clark. In 1877, Clarence H. Clark became president. One of its earlier partners was Jay Cooke, who left the firm in 1857 to start his own banking house, Jay Cooke and Company. In addition to its railroad investments, the Clark company developed railroads, particularly in the East. The company viewed the SVRR as an opportunity to open the western slopes of the Blue Ridge for the production of iron, coal, and gypsum. With this objective, they purchased the Satterlee construction and equipment contract, organized the Shenandoah Valley Construction Company, and named Kimball its president and chairman. Other officers of the construction company included Clarence H. Clark and Frederick S. Kimball, Kimball's father and Milnes' brother-in-law. The Clark company's long-range objective was to extend the SVRR into North Carolina,[66] a departure from the SVRR's 1872 decision to stop the railroad at Waynesboro.

The directors made two important financial decisions at a meeting in Charles Town on September 29.[67] The first was to issue $400,000 of income bonds, each bond valued at $1,000, paying six percent interest annually, beginning January 1, 1879, and maturing January 1, 1899. Interest was to be paid semi-annually with the principal paid at maturity at the office of the Clark company. The purposes of the bonds were to comply with the terms of the construction contract and to finance the equipping of the additional work force needed to complete the railroad to the C&O at the earliest possible date. Interest on the bonds was to be paid out of the railroad's income, including profit, but only after payment of operation and maintenance costs, interest, and other liabilities that had been incurred prior to the issuance of the income bonds.

The directors' second decision was to issue $1,500,000 of second mortgage bonds previously authorized by the stockholders in June 1871.

On November 18, the directors granted the construction company permission to use the SVRR's name when operating the road. The construction contract was modified to eliminate the extension from Shepherdstown to Beddington Station and to replace it with the extension from Shepherdstown to Hagerstown and a direct connection to the Cumberland Valley main line. The legality of the Hagerstown extension was questioned, however, and the company's legal counsel was directed to present proposals to the Maryland, West Virginia, and Virginia legislatures for its approval. The directors also approved borrowing funds from the Clark company.[68]

The highlight of 1879 occurred in December when trains began operating between Shepherdstown on the Potomac River and Riverton on the north side of the Shenandoah River near Front Royal, a distance of 42 miles.[69] Later that month, a contract was sublet to Mills and Rowland to grade the roadbed between Luray and the Shenandoah Iron Works at a cost not to exceed $50,000.[70]

1880

Accelerated construction activity and the equipping of the road for an increased level of operations continued. Activity by the officers and directors was intense. On January 20, the Shenandoah Valley Construction Company contract was modified to include the Shepherdstown-Hagerstown extension. This followed approval by the Maryland legislature. Plans for the extension, the bridge across the Potomac at Shepherdstown, and the location from Luray to the Shenandoah

Iron Works were approved. Also approved were the sale of bonds for the purchase of right-of-way, and payment of other claims against the company. The SVRR moved the sale of bonds and payment of bond interest to the Clark company's offices, with sales from other locations discontinued.[71]

The Virginia Midland Railroad, a subsidiary of the B&O, had brought suit against the SVRR over the grade crossing of its Manassas branch at the Shenandoah River. The suit was withdrawn when an agreement was reached on the rates to be charged for interchanging traffic between the two railroads. As part of the settlement, the SVRR agreed to bypass Front Royal and locate its road along the South Fork of the Shenandoah River.[72]

Other matters covered in the January 20 meeting were the designation of Kimball as the company's representative to receive payments for carrying mail, and the lease of three locomotives, two first-class passenger coaches, two combination smoking/baggage cars, 31 box cars, 10 gondolas, and 7 flat cars from the Railroad Equipment Company for $55,083.[73]

On February 4, a special stockholders' meeting was held in Winchester.[74] The two largest stockholders represented were Shenandoah Valley Construction, 8,000 shares, and Central Improvement, 5,000 shares. The Central Improvement holdings indicated that the Pennsylvania Railroad still retained an interest in the SVRR, but not to a level that could override management decisions by E. W. Clark and Company.

Milnes reported rapid construction progress: steel rails had been purchased, the bridge over the Shenandoah River at Riverton was nearing completion, and the contract for the Shepherdstown-Hagerstown extension had been sublet to the Borst Construction Company. The Potomac River bridge at Shepherdstown had been sublet to the firm of Confrade Saylor for approximately $57,000. The bridge consisted of five 167-foot spans,[75] with completion scheduled for July 1. The road from Hagerstown to the Shenandoah Iron Works, 107 miles, was scheduled for completion by fall, with the remainder into Waynesboro, 37 miles, to be completed by the end of 1880. The schedule was contingent on the Maryland legislature allowing the Shenandoah Valley to issue first mortgage bonds at $15,000 per mile for the 16 miles of work in Maryland.

Communications were received from Port Republic in Rockingham County and from Waynesboro. Waynesboro was concerned with the location of the depot and the junction with the C&O. The SVRR had been disappointed with Waynesboro's support and located the depot north of the town.[76]

The meeting was not without controversy. A. W. McDonald from Clarke County, a stockholder and former director, objected to the settlement with Central Improvement, by which it had received $1,392,000 of SVRR securities under what he believed was a void contract. He proposed a resolution repudiating the settlement. Milnes, Boyce, and Travers moved to table the resolution, which carried 2,312 shares to 901 shares. Central

Shenandoah Valley Construction Train

Back row, left to right, **Upton Boyce, Foster Morse, Clarence H. Clark, D. W. Flickwir, Joseph Sands, and William Milnes, Jr.**

Special Collections Department, University Libraries of Virginia Tech

Improvement abstained. Milnes and Boyce had been authorized to settle with the construction company four years earlier (April 10, 1876) on terms approved by the directors.

On April 6, the directors met at Shepherdstown[77] and agreed to establish and staff an office in Philadelphia to conduct the company's business. The treasurer, William G. McDonald of Philadelphia, replaced Kimball as the agent to receive payments for carrying mail in Maryland, West Virginia, and Virginia.

The Clark company agreed to accept $250,000 of second mortgage bonds for an equal amount of first mortgage bonds that it owned, making the first mortgage bonds available to the SVRR for payments to the contractor.

A modification to the February 3, 1876, traffic contract with the Cumberland Valley was approved. The two railroads had been negotiating for an extended period and with the SVRR nearing completion, the need for a permanent traffic agreement was critical.

The annual stockholders' meeting was held at Winchester on May 5.[78] The largest stockholder present was Shenandoah Valley Construction, 10,500 shares, represented by Kimball. Milnes reported that the bridge over the Shenandoah River at Riverton had been completed and placed in operation on April 1, providing 56 miles of service between Shepherdstown and Bentonville, a small community 11 miles south of Front Royal. The Shepherdstown-Hagerstown section was scheduled for completion on July 1, with the

entire road from Hagerstown to Waynesboro completed and operating by September. The stockholders, after many years of disappointment, were obviously pleased with the amount of work accomplished and adopted a resolution of thanks to the construction company for the "prompt, efficient and satisfactory manner in which it had executed the terms of the agreement."

Other items of business included moving the general office from Charles Town to Luray and receipt of a communication from Winchester indicating interest in a connection to the SVRR. This connection never developed due to local opposition which preferred a connection to the Cumberland Valley.[79] Agreements to connect the SVRR to the C&O and the Cumberland Valley had been completed, although traffic agreements remained unresolved.

Page County's $200,000 bond subscription had become a problem since the board of supervisors had issued only $4,000 of the county's bonds. On July 24, Vice President Boyce and Director William Travers were authorized to demand that the county issue the remaining $196,000 of its subscription. The board of supervisors rejected the demand.[80]

While the road was not completed by September, significant increments of construction were completed and operations started. The construction company, working north from Waynesboro, reached Elkton in Rockingham County on November 22 and the Shenandoah Iron Works on December 20. The Shepherdstown-Hagerstown section had been completed on August 19, and the first train from Bentonville reached Hagerstown on September 4. Two of the railroad's early locomotives, Numbers 2 and 3, built by the Baldwin Locomotive Works, were named the William Milnes, Jr. and the U. L. Boyce.[81]

During the year Kimball and the Clark company became aware that the AM&O was for sale. Although it had been in receivership since 1875, it had continued as a well-equipped and well-maintained railroad and was a sound investment opportunity. Kimball was also aware of the vast coal deposits of southwestern Virginia and West Virginia. Acquisition of the AM&O would allow the Clark company to develop these deposits, at the same time enhancing its investment in the SVRR by connecting the two railroads. However, Kimball was unable to negotiate its purchase from the English bondholders, delaying its acquisition by the Clark company until 1881.[82]

1881, JANUARY THROUGH MAY 5

The most significant event in the history of the SVRR occurred on February 10, when E. W. Clark and Company acquired the AM&O for $8,605,000, plus assumption of liens and claims, which increased the total cost to about $15,500,000.[83] It was renamed the Norfolk and Western Railroad to assure Norfolk and eastern Virginia that they would remain a vital market for the reorganized railroad. On February 28, an extension of the SVRR south from Waynesboro to some convenient point on the AM&O, now the N&W, was approved.[84]

In March, the construction north from Waynesboro and south from Bentonville joined at Luray, and the completed railroad was accepted. Full operations began on April 18,[85] when the first train arrived in Waynesboro from Hagerstown.

April and May were extremely busy months for the officers. On April 1, a final settlement for the construction from Hagerstown to Waynesboro was negotiated with Shenandoah Valley Construction. The railroad proposed a settlement for $265,199 cash and $196,000 of the unissued Page County bonds. The county bonds were a sticking point. Kimball proposed the substitution of $125,000 of second mortgage bonds and 3,000 shares of paid-up capital stock for the Page County bonds. His proposal was accepted.[86]

President Milnes submitted his resignation at a special stockholders' meeting in Luray on April 4.[87] Kimball was elected as his replacement, making him president of both the railroad company and the construction company. U. L. Boyce continued as vice president, and Milnes and Clarence H. Clark, president of E. W. Clark and Company, were among the directors elected. The company announced publicly its intention to extend the railroad south from Waynesboro through Augusta, Rockbridge, Botetourt, and Roanoke Counties to a connection with the AM&O at or near Bonsack or some other convenient point of connection.

A contract with Shenandoah Valley Construction for construction of the extension was approved. W. W. Coe, the construction company's chief engineer, was named to the same position with the railroad company. Milnes, Clarence Clark, and U. L. Boyce were named to a Committee on Construction, with authority to resolve all matters regarding location, construction, and negotiation of mortgage bonds.

Other actions included an increase in capital to $6,000,000 and the receipt of a letter from Lynchburg requesting that it be made the point of intersection of the SVRR and the AM&O. The letter was referred to Kimball for whatever action he considered appropriate. His response, if any, is unknown.

At the annual stockholders' meeting in Luray on May 5,[88] President Kimball noted the completion of the road to Waynesboro and the execution of contracts with the Cumberland Valley, Pennsylvania, Western Maryland, and C&O Railroads, creating a through line to New York, Philadelphia, Baltimore, and to areas served by the C&O to the south and west. The Clark company's acquisition of the AM&O and its reorganization as the Norfolk and Western Railroad was announced.

A report outlining plans for the extension south from Waynesboro indicated that

- Location surveys had been conducted and a line established.
- The general location of the line followed along the western base of the Blue Ridge. From Waynesboro, it followed the Shenandoah River to its source, crossed the divide to a tributary of the north branch of the James

River to a point near Lexington (Buena Vista), where it connected to the Richmond and Allegheny Railroad. From Buena Vista, the line followed the north and south branches of the James River to Buchanan, then crossed the divide to Tinker Creek, which it followed to the N&W at Big Lick.

- Most of the right-of-way had been secured.
- Construction contracts had been awarded, work started, and steel rails and fasteners purchased.
- Work would be completed by the end of 1881.

The plan for financing the extension was based on an estimated cost of $2,250,000 for construction and the additional equipment required for expanded operations between Hagerstown and Big Lick. The Fidelity Insurance Trust and Safe Deposit Company of Philadelphia provided a general mortgage for $25,000 per mile, six percent, 40-year bonds applying to the total 238-mile length of the line, yielding $5,950,000. Three million, five hundred and sixty-two thousand dollars would be used to retire the bonds outstanding on the Hagerstown-Waynesboro section, with the balance of $2,388,000 available for constructing and equipping the extension into Big Lick. This mortgage had been authorized by the stockholders at the special April 4 meeting in Luray.

The treasurer reported the company's assets at $6,633,455 and liabilities of the same amount. Included in the liabilities were capital stock, $2,508,700; first mortgage loans, $2,137,000; second mortgage income loans, $1,425,000; and, equipment notes for rolling stock, $323,152.

LOCAL ACTIVITIES IN THE SELECTION OF THE POINT OF CONNECTION, APRIL 4 THROUGH APRIL 22

The most important part of Kimball's May 5 annual report was the designation of Big Lick as the connecting point for the SVRR and the N&W. This decision had been made sometime between April 4, when Bonsack was identified as the connecting point, and May 5.

The SVRR considered Salem, Big Lick, Bonsack, and Montvale as potential locations for its connection to the N&W. Salem was the county seat, had the largest population and greatest political influence, and was the location of Roanoke College. Big Lick, Bonsack, and Montvale were small villages located along the N&W in Roanoke and Bedford Counties. For the community selected, its future growth, economic development and prosperity would be assured. There was, therefore, keen competition between the four communities to influence the SVRR to decide in their favor.

An examination of each community's efforts during the April 4–May 5 period when the SVRR made its selection decision reveals the reasons the Committee on Construction selected Big Lick rather than one of the other communities.

The Construction Committee had been authorized to resolve all matters regarding location, construction, and financing. They would be responsible for selecting the location for the SVRR-N&W connection. Their decision would be based on the community whose location required minimum construction and right-of-way costs. Petitions by local politicians, businessmen, citizens, and elected officials were less important.

Over the years, the story has persisted that Salem was not interested in securing the connection of the two railroads, even to the point that Salem's leaders either ignored or made themselves unavailable when SVRR engineers visited the town in early 1881. There is no evidence to support this view. Salem, as a college town and business and political center, was vitally interested in securing the connection. The SVRR was Salem's last opportunity to obtain a direct railroad connection to the North, for in 1879, Roanoke County had refused to complete its $200,000 subscription to the VRR, even though substantial construction had been completed and right-of-way purchased from Salem east to the Botetourt County line.

Salem's efforts began with a presentation to the SVRR stockholders at their April 4 meeting in Luray. The Salem delegation, headed by Dr. Julius Dreher, president of Roanoke College, requested that Salem be selected as the point of connection. The delegation set forth Salem's merits but at the same time acknowledged that it was located several miles west of Big Lick. Dr. Dreher was optimistic about Salem's chances. On his return from Luray, he expressed the opinion that Salem would be selected. Failing to receive any response to its April 4 presentation, Salem submitted a petition on April 28 to U.S. Senator William Mahone requesting his assistance in obtaining the connection point. The petition was signed by numerous business leaders, town officials, and influential citizens.

On April 30, Senator Mahone forwarded the petition to President Kimball, accompanied by his personal observation that Salem was the preferred point of connection.[89] It is not known if Kimball responded to Mahone's letter, but by April 30, Big Lick may have already been selected.

Salem's disadvantage was its location. Although the SVRR's charter specified that the connection be located at or near Salem, this did not ensure its selection. The distance from Cloverdale to Salem, following the VRR right-of-way, is approximately four miles longer than the Cloverdale to Big Lick branch. Salem's selection would have increased the Shenandoah Valley's mortgage by $100,000 and added the cost of constructing four additional miles of railroad. Acquisition of right-of-way, either that owned by the Valley Railroad or along a new location, would have been another added cost. It is obvious why Salem was not selected.

Montvale was not a serious candidate. Montvale's disadvantage was its location on the opposite side of the Blue Ridge Mountains from the SVRR mainline. Although it would have shortened the length of the main line substantially, a branch line to the N&W required a difficult and costly tunnel crossing under conditions comparable to those Claudius Crozet and Claibourne R. Mason faced in the Virginia Central Railroad tunnel crossing of the Blue Ridge at Rockfish Gap in 1857.

Of the remaining communities, Bonsack held the advantage over Big Lick. At the April 4 stockholders' meeting SVRR officers specifically identified Bonsack as a location for the N&W connection. The accompanying map illustrates Bonsack's advantage. From a common point on the SVRR main line, a branch line to the N&W at Bonsack would have been about five miles long as compared to approximately eight and one-half miles required for a connection at Big Lick. The shorter distance reduced significantly the construction and right-of-way costs required by the Big Lick connection. One negative feature of the Bonsack branch line may have been the steeper grades and heavier excavation required to cross the ridges paralleling the north sides of Coyner and Read Mountains. Even so, Bonsack was a serious candidate.

Big Lick faced an uphill battle in its effort to secure the SVRR-N&W connection. Bonsack's economic advantage and its April 4 designation as the likely connection point had to be overcome. Numerous discussions were held in the community in early April as to how the connection point could be obtained. At a town meeting on April 21,[90] John C. Moomaw stepped forward and suggested that a monetary contribution to the railroad company would advance their cause. Moomaw was a right-of-way agent or consultant for the SVRR,[91] as well as a successful orchardist and astute businessman.

As right-of-way agent, Moomaw knew the specific locations of the routes being considered, the point at which each connected to the N&W, and the properties needed for the railroad right-of-way. His job was to contact the affected property owners, negotiate a price for their property, and obtain an

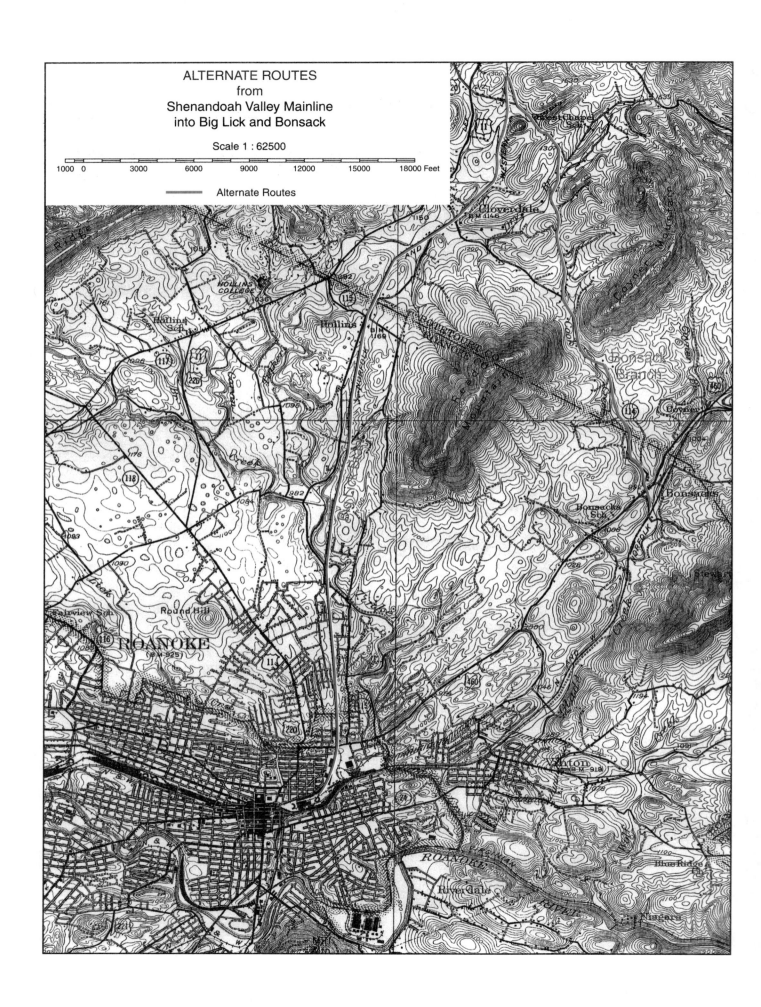

option for its purchase by the railroad company. If the negotiated price was acceptable, the SVRR would exercise the option, prepare a deed formalizing the purchase, and record it in the Clerk of the Circuit Court's Office. The actual deed would then be delivered to Moomaw for transmittal to the railroad company.

Roanoke County deed books indicate that Moomaw was involved in this process for 12 parcels purchased by the SVRR for its right-of-way into Big Lick. By sometime in April, Moomaw had completed the work. On May 9, Kimball had a sketch showing the results of his efforts. The sketch identified the "locations of parcels near Big Lick on which options of purchase have been secured." Kimball referred this information to the Committee on Construction with "the power to acquire property at Big Lick or other points."

Moomaw was therefore able to advise Big Lick's leaders[92] on how they could secure the SVRR-N&W connection. He proposed a monetary contribution. Different accounts of the April 21 meeting give the amount of the contribution as $5,000, $7,500, or $10,000. Moomaw's advice for an appropriate amount may have been based on the total purchase price for the 12 right-of-way parcels on which he had negotiated purchase options. Based on the average purchase price for 7 of these parcels, as recorded in Roanoke County deed books, the total purchase price for all 12 parcels was $7,500.

Moomaw's decision to share his knowledge of location and right-of-way costs with

Big Lick rather than Bonsack is intriguing. Moomaw was originally from Bonsack but moved to Cloverdale in 1859. His orchards and packing houses were located on the SVRR's proposed route into Big Lick, and direct railroad access would benefit his orchard business. In addition, one of the right-of-way parcels required for the Big Lick route was owned by Lucinda Moomaw, his daughter. Regardless of Moomaw's reasons for advising Big Lick or the actual amount of the contribution, his advice was accepted, the money was raised, and arrangements were made for its delivery.

From this point, there are two variations of the story. The first has Charles W. Thomas delivering the subscription to a directors' meeting in Lexington. However, the SVRR minutes do not indicate that a directors' meeting was ever held in Lexington.

The second and more likely scenario has Thomas meeting Moomaw north of Troutville late in the evening of April 21 and turning the contribution over to him. From here, Moomaw made an all-night horseback ride to Lexington. He arrived on the 22nd and delivered the Big Lick subscription and the right-of-way options he had negotiated to the Committee on Construction. Upon receipt of this information, U. L. Boyce, a committee member, responded, "Gentlemen, this brings the road to Big Lick. This progressive spirit cannot be denied."[93]

The Committee on Construction was likely in Lexington on their way to the Roanoke Valley to finalize the location for connecting the two railroads. With Moomaw's information, the selection decision was made and the need to continue into the Roanoke Valley was no longer necessary. The committee then returned to Luray, reported to Kimball the receipt of Moomaw's options for right-of-way near Big Lick, the Big Lick contribution for purchase of the right-of-way, and their recommendation to select Big Lick. Kimball then incorporated their recommendation in his May 5 report, advising the stockholders that the SVRR would connect to the N&W at Big Lick.

COMMITTEE ON CONSTRUCTION ACTIVITIES AFTER APRIL 22

The directors met in Philadelphia on May 9.[94] The Committee on Construction reported that Chief Engineer W. W. Coe's plans and estimates for the Waynesboro-Big Lick extension had been approved and contractors requested to submit proposals for its construction. The work was divided into sections, and 13 contractors were employed on the 95-mile extension.

Other committee actions included a recommendation that the main line be terminated at Cloverdale and a branch line constructed to Big Lick. This recommendation circumvented the 1867 charter requirement to make connection to the then Virginia and Tennessee at or near Salem. By stopping the main line at Cloverdale and constructing a branch line into Big Lick, a distance of approximately six and one-half miles, the SVRR was in compliance with the April 1870 Act of the General Assembly authorizing construction of branch and lateral roads not

exceeding 10 miles in length. The committee further recommended that a survey be conducted for an extension to Rocky Mount, confirming the Clark company's intent to ultimately extend the road into North Carolina.

Following the Committee on Construction's report, Kimball gave them the sketch of the right-of-way parcels required for the Big Lick connection for their acquisition of property at Big Lick and other locations.

Following the May 9 meeting, the Committee on Construction purchased the 12 right-of-way parcels. The deeds for these parcels were executed between May 30 and August 5, 1881, recorded in the Roanoke County Clerk's Office, and delivered to John C. Moomaw.

Moomaw was the local person responsible for the SVRR's decision to connect its railroad to the N&W at Big Lick.[95] His foresight and business ability in recognizing that a monetary contribution was the most important factor in the SVRR's selection process proved invaluable. As a result of John C. Moomaw's advice to the Big Lick community, a "Magic City" was born on April 22, 1881.

1881, JUNE THROUGH DECEMBER

By June, construction from Waynesboro to Big Lick was progressing rapidly. During the month, an agreement with Luray to locate shops there fell through when it declined to purchase the company's stock.[96] On July 25, the long-running effort to have Page County fulfill its commitment to issue bonds for the purchase of stock was resolved. The settlement provided that Page County complete its subscription by turning over to the railroad $200,000 of its bonds in return for $200,000 of stock. The stock was then sold by the county to the Clark Company for $100,000. The settlement agreement was completed on August 27 and confirmed by the Virginia General Assembly on April 22, 1882. The Clark Company was the obvious beneficiary of the settlement, although Page County was able to reduce its commitment by $100,000.[97]

An event which would later prove significant in the development of Big Lick occurred on August 3, when the Roanoke Machine Works were organized. Its principal office was at Big Lick and its officers were Frederick J. Kimball, president, George R. W. Armes, secretary, and W. G. MacDowell, treasurer. Directors were Clarence H. Clark, George F. Tyler, U. L. Boyce, E. W. Clark, Jr., William A. Travers and Peyton L. Terry. All were from Philadelphia except Boyce from Clarke County, Travers from Jefferson County, and Terry from Roanoke County.[98]

On August 20, the town of Buchanan passed an ordinance allowing the Shenandoah Valley to use its streets and alleys for railroad operations. Train speeds could not exceed six miles per hour and engineers were required to ring their locomotive bells when passing through town.[99]

At a special meeting in Philadelphia on September 6,[100] Kimball changed the form of the stock certificate being used to the certificate illustrated on the following page and directed that condemnation of right-of-way along the Waynesboro-Big Lick extension be avoided. This may have been an effort to avoid the ill feelings inherent in the condemnation process and to avoid construction delays.

At a special directors' meeting in Philadelphia on October 19,[101] President Kimball announced the organization of the Roanoke Machine Works. The Works were capitalized at $250,000, with 70 percent of the stock subscribed by the N&W and 30 percent by the Shenandoah Valley. The Works were a separate concern whose purpose was to construct and equip machine shops large enough to build first-class locomotives. As a result, the shops at Shepherdstown were closed.

Other business included the execution of a traffic agreement between the N&W, the SVRR, and the East Tennessee, Virginia, and Georgia Railroad.[102] With this agreement, Thomas A. Scott's vision of a railroad extending from Pennsylvania to Alabama through the Great Appalachian Valley was realized.

1882

On May 5, Kimball described[103] to the stockholders the problems in locating and constructing the 95-mile extension and the manner in which they had been resolved "with a clarity highly creditable to the contractors employed and to the engineers engaged in the service of your company."

1881 Shenandoah Valley Railroad Stock Certificate

Shenandoah Valley Railroad Company Stockholders and Directors Minute Book A

His report indicated that

- the entire line would be in operation by June 15,

- the line connected to the Richmond and Allegheny Railroad 43 miles south of Waynesboro, where the iron ores of the James River Valley would be interchanged to the SVRR, thereby providing an outlet to the Pennsylvania furnaces,

- the workshops at Roanoke were under construction and designed for the joint use of the SVRR and the N&W and,

- the line would serve the Shenandoah Iron Company (Works), under the management of William Milnes, Jr., former president, who had started construction of a 100-ton per-day furnace to produce pig iron. Completion was scheduled for the summer.

Kimball's reference to Roanoke was one of the first in the SVRR's records, the town having received its charter in February 1882.

Milnes' continuing influence in the SVRR's affairs was confirmed when Kimball decided to operate the railroad in two divisions. This required that engine houses and repair shops be located at the Shenandoah Iron Works, a point nearly equidistant between Hagerstown and Roanoke. These shops were erected and in use by May.

Following the stockholders' meeting President Kimball named the company's officers: U. L. Boyce, vice president; William J. McDowell, treasurer; George Armes, secretary; William H. Travers, general counsel; Joseph Durand, Philadelphia, solicitor; W. W. Coe, Roanoke, chief engineer; Charles Blackwell, Roanoke, superintendent of machine works; Joseph Sands, Hagerstown, superintendent; and Joseph W. Coxe, Hagerstown, auditor and general ticket agent.

The Shenandoah Valley Railroad was completed on June 19, when the first through train arrived in Roanoke from Hagerstown, just four days behind the scheduled June 15 completion date.[104]

With the naming of officers and the beginning of operations between Hagerstown and Roanoke, the SVRR, after 15 difficult and arduous years, was complete. With the assistance of the Pennsylvania Railroad in its early years and with the financial, management, and construction support of E. W. Clark and Company from 1879, the SVRR had won the battle to create a north-south railroad through the Valley of Virginia and, at the same time, had provided the impetus which led to the founding of Roanoke, the "Magic City."

EPILOGUE

The SVRR's triumph was not without price. In its first report to the Virginia Railroad Commissioner on December 13, 1883, a funded debt of $7,961,000 was reported, represented by three separate mortgages bearing an average interest rate of five percent. Under these mortgages, $536,000 of the bonds issued were held by the SVRR as assets, $333,066 of which were secured as collateral. The cost of constructing and equipping the railroad was represented by the total issue of the capital stock, $3,696,200, and the total funded debt, $7,961,000, a total of $11,657,200.

Motive power and rolling stock consisted of 32 locomotives, 18 first-class passenger cars, 12 baggage, mail, express cars, and 819 freight cars, supported by 795 employees and 5 engine houses and shops.

With revenues exceeding expenses by $128,752, 1883 was a successful year. However, in the following year, the company was unable to pay the interest on its mortgages, and on April 1, 1885, the company was placed in the hands of a receiver, Sydney F. Tyler of Philadelphia. On December 15, 1890, the Shenandoah Valley Railroad passed into history when it was purchased by Clarence H. Clark and conveyed to the N&W, the SVRR's majority stockholder.[105]

Chapter IV
A History of the Valley Railroad, 1866–1881

1866–1871

The Valley Railroad was incorporated by the Virginia General Assembly on February 23, 1866.[1] The charter was to become effective when $100,000 of the $3,000,000 authorized capital had been subscribed. This occurred in October 1866 when Rockbridge County passed a $100,000 bond issue for the purchase of stock priced at $100 a share. The railroad was to begin at Harrisonburg, proceed south through Rockingham County, pass through Staunton, Augusta County, Lexington, Rockbridge County, Buchanan, Fincastle, and Botetourt County, and terminate at or near Salem in Roanoke County with a connection to the Virginia and Tennessee Railroad, a total distance of 113 miles. The charter specified that the railroad could not be completed within 20 miles of the Virginia and Tennessee until one year after the completion of the Covington and Ohio Railroad, an extension of the Virginia Central Railroad. The Covington and Ohio was completed to Huntington, West Virginia, on January 29, 1873, as the Chesapeake

and Ohio Railroad. The earliest possible completion date for the VRR was therefore January 29, 1874.

Depots were to be located in Lexington on North River Navigation Company land and at Buchanan on James River and Kanawha Canal Company land. Books for stock subscription were opened at six locations along the proposed route, and commissioners were named to receive subscriptions.

In April 1866, an organizing convention was held in Staunton,[2] with Harrisonburg, Staunton, Lexington, and the counties of Rockingham, Augusta, Rockbridge, Botetourt, and Roanoke represented. Plans and benefits to each community were discussed, and the capital each county would have to raise to make the project possible was established. Colonel Michael G. Harman of Staunton served as chairman of the convention and was elected the first president, together with ten directors.

Michael G. Harman was a farmer and entrepreneur and one of the wealthiest men in the Shenandoah Valley. He was born in Waynesboro in August 1823 and was one of five Harman brothers, all outstanding citizens of Augusta County. Prior to the Civil War, Harman ran the Virginia Hotel in Staunton and operated stage and freight lines with his brother Asher. Harman was a stockholder of the Virginia Central Railroad and a director of the Central Bank in Staunton.

At the beginning of the Civil War, he was second in command of the 52nd Virginia Infantry, a regiment comprised primarily of volunteers from Augusta County. Harman was promoted to colonel and assumed command of the 52nd on May 1, 1862. He was wounded in the same month at the Battle of McDowell. He returned to duty after recovering from his wounds but resigned in June 1863 because of disability. Harman then served as quartermaster at Staunton for the remainder of the war. Following the war, he resumed his stage and freight line business, was a leader in organizing the Valley Railroad, and served as its president until August 30, 1870. Thereafter, he served on its board of directors.[3]

With Virginia's economy in disarray following the Civil War, the VRR, like the SVRR, was a remarkable and optimistic undertaking. Although Staunton and Salem had railroad service in 1866, Harrisonburg, Rockingham County, Lexington, Rockbridge County, Buchanan, Fincastle, and Botetourt County did not. For Lexington and Buchanan, the only available public transportation was provided by the North River and James River and Kanawha Canal companies. Canal systems

throughout the United States were being replaced by the more efficient railroads, and the VRR was visualized as an important economic development project, needed for the area to recover its pre-Civil War prosperity. Its potential for economic development was limited however, unless it could be connected to an existing railroad which served the northern and midwestern markets needed by the valley's agricultural products, mineral resources, and passenger service requirements.

The existing railroads which would connect to the VRR at Staunton and Salem were east-west operations providing limited connections to the important northern and midwestern markets. This limitation was recognized soon after the organizing convention. In June 1866, Harman and several directors approached the Manassas Gap Railroad to seek an arrangement to use its tracks between Strasburg and Mount Jackson and to transfer its authority to build the sections between Mount Jackson and Harrisonburg and between Strasburg and Winchester. This arrangement would connect the VRR to the existing Winchester and Potomac Railroad which was controlled by the B&O. It connected Winchester to the B&O main line at Harpers Ferry.

The negotiations were inconclusive,[4] and on March 1, 1867, the General Assembly amended the VRR's charter to allow it to construct and equip a continuous line from the terminal point on the Virginia and Tennessee through the main Shenandoah Valley, by or near the towns of New Market, Woodstock, and Winchester. The VRR was authorized to purchase, lease, manage, or work any existing railroad along such line and to construct one or more railroads from Winchester to the Potomac River.[5]

This legislation provided the VRR greater flexibility and leverage in its negotiations with the Manassas Gap and Winchester and Potomac Railroads, although the authority to build a railroad parallel to the Winchester and Potomac would place it in direct competition with the B&O.

The VRR had no reason to compete with the B&O since it had supported the VRR's planning activities from its beginning. In 1866, at Harman's request, James L. Randolph, then a B&O civil engineer, conducted a preliminary location survey for the 113-mile railroad from Harrisonburg to Salem at a cost of $1,800. The findings of his survey were reported at the VRR's 1867 annual meeting.[6]

At the same time the VRR was seeking a means to extend its railroad from Harrisonburg to Winchester, the B&O was attempting to accomplish the same objective.

John W. Garrett, like his rival, Thomas A. Scott, had long visualized a railroad through the Valley of Virginia as one means of extending his railroad into the South. Garrett had begun this effort prior to the Civil War by using the Winchester and Potomac to provide rail service to the lower Shenandoah Valley.

In 1866, the B&O leased the Winchester and Potomac for 99 years and began to purchase stock in the Orange and Alexandria Railroad, which in March 1867 was combined with the Manassas Gap Railroad. The combined company, the Orange, Alexandria and Manassas Gap, was authorized to extend its existing railroad from Mount Jackson to Harrisonburg. With the financial support of the B&O, the extension was completed in December 1868 as the Strasburg and Harrisonburg Railroad. In March 1870, the Winchester and Strasburg Railroad, in which the B&O was the majority stockholder, opened for service.[7]

Through these activities, the B&O had extended its system to Harrisonburg, eliminating the need for the VRR to use its March 1867 legislative authority to lease or build the railroads between Winchester and Harrisonburg. By March 1870, the only unfinished link in a railroad connecting the B&O main line at Harpers Ferry to the Virginia and Tennessee at Salem was the 113-mile Harrisonburg to Salem segment.

With the VRR having the legal authority to construct this segment, it was logical for the B&O to become involved in its development by providing financial aid, engineering, equipment, and operating personnel. While there is no specific evidence of a formal joint effort agreement, it is apparent that sometime after March 1867, the VRR and the B&O concluded that a partnership would be mutually advantageous.

Efforts to raise capital in the sponsoring communities proceeded slowly. On November 16, 1868, the citizens of Roanoke County requested that voters be polled on the question of Roanoke County participation in the

VRR. It was not until May 1870 that the poll was actually taken to subscribe $200,000 to the railroad company and to issue bonds redeemable in 20 years. The voters approved the bonds, contingent on the road being extended to the center of the county, with the funds derived expended only in Roanoke County. The supervisors did not authorize issuance of the bonds until December 1870. They later nullified this action, but on May 17, 1873, the supervisors reconsidered, clearing the way for the execution and delivery of $200,000 of Roanoke County bonds to the B&O.[8]

Bond subscriptions in Rockbridge County likewise reflected concerns on how the funds raised would be used. Rockbridge approved three separate bond issues in 1866, 1868, and 1871, totaling $525,000. Each issue contained conditions requiring that $1,000,000 of the VRR's capital be contributed by the city of Baltimore since it would be the prime beneficiary of the VRR. The Rockbridge conditions also specified that its bonds would not be delivered until construction in the county had begun.[9]

Botetourt County also attached conditions to its $200,000 subscription, and in Augusta County, bond subscriptions were rejected by the voters in 1870 and again in 1871.[10] The only subscriptions without conditions were the Staunton and Lexington issues. Clearly, the participating communities were concerned with the overall financing of the project and the extent to which the B&O and the city of Baltimore would participate financially.

By 1869 it was apparent that the local communities would be unable to fully finance the railroad, and a delegation traveled to Baltimore to formally request that city's financial aid. On April 23, the delegation, with Robert E. Lee as its spokesman, appeared before the Baltimore Board of Trade, where President Harman requested the board to endorse $1,000,000 in construction aid, with the counties and towns being served contributing $1,200,000. Harman noted that construction would not be possible without this aid. The delegation presented the same request to the city council, with Lee observing that "this route will afford the shortest line of travel from the large and populous portion of the North to much of the best part of the South." The council acted favorably on the request, although the aid required approval by the Maryland legislature and the Baltimore electorate, a time-consuming process which delayed the start of construction.[11]

By August 1870, the conditions by which the city of Baltimore's financial aid would become available had not been resolved. Only slightly more than 7,000 shares of stock had been subscribed: 4,000 shares by Rockbridge County, 2,000 shares by Botetourt County, and 1,000 shares by Staunton. Fifty-one shares were subscribed by 29 private investors.[12]

President Harman, the driving force in organizing the railroad, was discouraged by the difficulties in raising capital and declined to stand for re-election at the August 1870 stockholders' meeting. He believed that some special emphasis was necessary to make investment in the VRR more attractive. He proposed that Lee succeed him as president, believing that only a person of his character, reputation, influence, and stature could inspire confidence and provide the credibility needed to make the railroad a success.[13] Lee was then president of Washington College.

Since the surrender at Appomattox, Lee had declined to participate in any business enterprise. On July 25, 1870, President Harman, John B. Baldwin, Judge Hugh Sheffey, Alexander H. H. Stuart, Thomas I. Michie and other citizens and community leaders asked Lee to accept the presidency of the VRR, convincing him that he alone could make the company a successful service to the Valley of Virginia, Lexington, and Washington College.

On July 28, Lee indicated his willingness to accept the office, and at the stockholders' meeting on August 30, 1870, Lee was formally elected the company's second president.[14] His acceptance of the presidency was typical of his unselfish peacetime service to the Commonwealth of Virginia and Washington College. His quiet, unassuming behind-the-scenes counsel and advice on the political questions of the day were influential in Virginia's post-war recovery. He was instrumental in healing the bitterness dividing the North and the South.

In 1867, when Virginia was Military District No. 1, an election was held to select delegates to a convention to write a new state constitution. Many white voters questioned the need to participate, assuming their votes would be meaningless in the likelihood that the election would result in radical control of the convention. Lee, acting discreetly, advised participation in the election and active citizenship in all matters to facilitate reunification of the nation and the healing of all dissensions. Lee also advocated a system of state-wide public education which did not exist at that time. Although the radicals prevailed in the election, the resulting constitution provided for public education.[15]

As president of Washington College, Lee conducted his final campaign, one with farreaching and lasting impact, one that was more successful than any of his military battles and strategies. His vision, leadership, and desire to bring together a divided people led to the college becoming a national institution, a place for educating young men from both North and South. During the five years of his presidency, the curriculum was broadened to include a law school, programs in business instruction, and courses in journalism. He was able to enlarge the school's financial resources through the contributions of men such as Cyrus McCormick, inventor of the reaper and a Rockbridge County native, and Thomas P. Scott, a Pennsylvanian who had served in Lincoln's cabinet.[16]

Unfortunately, Lee's term as the VRR's president was brief. Following his death on October 12, 1870, Robert Garrett was named the railroad's third president. Garrett was the son of John W. Garrett. His family, originally Baltimore bankers, controlled the B&O from 1858 to 1887. Robert Garrett attended Princeton College and began his career with the B&O as assistant to the president. He had little practical experience in financing, constructing, or operating a railroad. He served as the VRR's president until February 1875, taking a sabbatical until October 1879 when he returned to the B&O. Following the death of his father in October 1884, he was elected president of the B&O and served until October 1887, when the B&O's financial problems ended his administration.[17]

Garrett's election indicated that the B&O was in control of the VRR. The capitalization of the VRR was still incomplete and by the fall of 1871 only the B&O's subscription of $1,000,000 was firm. The city of Baltimore's $1,000,000 subscription remained conditional, and the local communities had not met their $1,200,000 goal. Meeting this goal was necessary to secure the Baltimore subscription, but only $1,105,000 had been subscribed, leaving a shortfall of $95,000. To overcome this deficit, the B&O increased its commitment by $20,000, making it the VRR's largest stockholder. On August 1, 1871, a Staunton contracting firm, McMahon and Green, agreed to purchase $75,000 of the company's stock. These two actions eliminated the $95,000 shortfall, removing one of the conditions attached to the Baltimore subscription.

The McMahon and Green stock purchase was essentially a loan because their stock was to be purchased by future investors. In addition, McMahon and Green were to be repaid if Baltimore failed to meet its commitment.[18]

Although financing was not complete, planning and construction was proceeding. On November 29, 1871, James L. Randolph, acting for the VRR, was directed to have the railroad's route from Staunton via Fairfield to Lexington located and ready for construction by March 1, 1872.

1872

The directors met in early March 1872 and named Randolph chief engineer. He was instructed to place the work from Staunton to Salem under contract after a careful survey through Rockbridge County. For the 26-mile Harrisonburg-Staunton segment, Randolph was authorized to contract for several miles of the line, including bridges. The remaining work was to be placed under contract after Garrett's approval.

A bid by the McMahon and Green Company to build 30 miles of railroad between Staunton and Salem, with 20 percent of the work to be paid in bonds of the local communities, was considered. The local communities were unwilling to release these bonds until the entire 87-mile Staunton to Salem section was placed under contract. The McMahon and Green bid was rejected.[19]

On August 6, Randolph responded to the March directives with the following report:

- From Staunton to Salem, 87 miles, two lines had been located between Buchanan and Salem, but the work was incomplete. From Buchanan to Lexington 12 miles had been located with surveys continuing to Staunton.
- From Harrisonburg to Staunton, 26 miles, the heavy sections of the line and all bridges were under contract to six or seven contractors.[20]

President Garrett's first annual report cited difficulty in financing construction due to the many conditions imposed by the city of Baltimore and the local communities on the issuance of bonds and purchase of stock.[21] The treasurer's report indicated receipts of

$386,777, disbursements of $93,552, leaving a balance of $293,224. Garrett indicated that the "pecuniary means of prosecuting the work thus far have been chiefly derived from the contributions of the B&O, the conditions in connection with the other subscriptions, except those of Staunton and Lexington, not having as yet been complied with."

In addition to the difficulties encountered in arranging financing, Garrett's report included a request to examine the practicality of a route through central Botetourt County, eliminating direct service to Fincastle, the county seat. Randolph had found it difficult to select one of the two routes mentioned in his August 6 report. Final selection would not be resolved until 1876.

1873

Garrett's second annual report described in glowing terms the year's accomplishments. Highlights included:

- The conditional stock subscription by the city of Baltimore for $1,000,000 had been finalized on May 29, with this amount being made available at the same rate the other subscribers made their subscriptions available.
- The B&O had obtained control of the Strasburg and Harrisonburg, the Winchester and Strasburg and the Winchester and Potomac Railroads and was operating them.
- The chief engineer's estimate of the cost of the 113 miles of railroad, Harrisonburg to Salem, was $5,700,000.
- The VRR's financing was based on $3,200,000 of stock, subscribed in cash and in county and municipal bonds, with a limited amount

by private subscription. In addition, a mortgage not to exceed $3,000,000 to secure bonds at seven percent interest, payable annually, had been executed.

- The work from Harrisonburg to Staunton was scheduled for completion by November, including the connection to the C&O at Staunton. Garrett referred to the C&O as being "destined, upon completion of its western connections, to become one of the great channels of travel and traffic between the East and the West, and which it is anticipated will act in harmony with the Valley Railroad, receiving from and conferring upon it abundant reciprocal benefits."
- A contract for constructing the 87 miles from Staunton to Salem had been awarded to the Mason Syndicate. Payment would be in county bonds, discounted 15 percent, plus accrued interest.[22]

Garrett also spoke eloquently of the "connection with the Virginia and Tennessee road at Salem, having opened to it the means of inter-communication with the great Southwest."

Randolph supplemented Garrett's report with the following information:

- The work from Staunton to Salem was to be completed in three years and had begun in early July in Rockbridge, Botetourt, and Roanoke Counties and "has been continuously prosecuted, the contractors proposing to gradually expand and perfect, during the winter, organization for extensive operation in the spring."
- Surveys were continuing from Buchanan south but the final location for the railroad in Botetourt County had not been determined.[23]

By fall, construction was underway, with completion of the ballasted roadway scheduled for July 1876. It was anticipated that rails could be laid, bridges completed, and operations started during 1877. There were, however, other problems that Garrett had not addressed and would later prove to have an adverse impact on the progress and completion of the railroad.

The first was the lack of traffic agreements with the C&O and the AM&O. Without these agreements, the VRR could not succeed. Negotiation of these agreements should have been Garrett's first priority. While Garrett had anticipated that the C&O would act "in harmony" with the VRR through the exchange of "mutual benefits," his report gives no indication that negotiations were being conducted.[24]

His reference to the destiny of the C&O upon completion of its western connections indicated a lack of knowledge of ongoing developments. The C&O had begun operations between Richmond and Huntington, West Virginia, on the Ohio River on January 29, 1873, nine months prior to his annual report to the stockholders. Further, Garrett's report did not mention the coal deposits located along its route.[25]

Garrett's reference to the connection to the Virginia and Tennessee was also unrealistic. He could not have been ignorant or unaware of its consolidation into the AM&O in 1870. The *Baltimore Gazette* had reported "that the time for making this [the VRR] a through route is past; others have secured the connections which the Baltimore and Ohio Railroad had hoped to get by the Valley Railroad."[26]

Garrett, as a B&O officer, had been aware of William Mahone's bitter opposition to the B&O and the Pennsylvania during the legislative battles over railroad consolidation and divestiture in 1867 and 1870. Only on terms favorable to Mahone could Garrett have negotiated a traffic agreement for the VRR. Garrett was either presenting an unrealistic view of the VRR's potential or he was misleading its stockholders, the B&O stockholders, and the city of Baltimore. Garrett's veracity and management abilities were questionable.

The plan for financing the VRR, in terms of stock subscriptions purchased by cash and interest-bearing county and municipal bonds, supplemented by a mortgage, was as follows:

Private subscriptions -	$	75,000
B&O Railroad Company -		1,020,000
City of Baltimore -		1,000,000
County/Municipal bonds		
Staunton	$150,000	
Lexington	30,000	
Rockbridge	525,000	
Botetourt	200,000	
Roanoke	200,000	
		1,105,000
Mortgage		3,000,000
Total Capital		$ 6,200,000 [27]

The county and municipal bonds, when authorized, were to be turned over to the B&O. With the bonds discounted 15 percent for payments to contractors, the total capital was reduced almost $160,000. This reduction, plus reliance on the mortgage for nearly 50 percent of the total capitalization, proved inadequate in meeting the VRR's financial needs.

The situation was further compromised by the lack of financial participation by Rockingham and Augusta Counties. By August 31, about $540,000 had been spent on construction between Harrisonburg and Staunton. With the requirement that the funds derived from the sale of county bonds be expended on construction within each county and with the city of Baltimore making its contribution available as the county subscriptions were received, the Harrisonburg-Staunton construction was funded entirely by the B&O. With this 26-mile segment still incomplete, funding of the 87-mile Staunton-Salem construction became completely dependent on obtaining the $3,000,000 mortgage.

The mortgage proved to be the weak point in the VRR's capitalization. For all the optimism expressed by Garrett in his second annual report, the concluding paragraphs of this report were ominous. The treasurer reported a cash balance of only $6,700, and Garrett recommended that an "additional call of 30 percent be made on the stockholders of the company" by November 3.[28] This proposal was not well received in Rockbridge, Botetourt, and Roanoke Counties. Each county had anticipated that bonds would be issued only in amounts necessary to make partial payments to the contractor as work was completed in their county.

As a result of the financial panic which had occurred in September 1873, the VRR was unable to find a market for the $3,000,000 mortgage. The B&O, while it was able to weather the resulting economic pressures, suffered continuing losses of traffic and revenue, preventing it from providing an offsetting investment of funds in the VRR.

1874

The year started well enough when trains began running between Harrisonburg and Staunton on March 3.[29] For the 87 miles south of Staunton, agents were purchasing a 100-foot wide right-of-way. Deeds were recorded throughout the year in Rockbridge, Botetourt, and Roanoke Counties. Right-of-way purchases in Rockbridge County had been recorded during the last three months of 1873, principally in the area north of Lexington. This pattern continued into January, but beginning in February and continuing through September, right-of-way purchases south of Lexington predominated. In Botetourt County, the majority of right-of-way purchases were recorded on the north and south ends of the line, comprising approximately one-half of the total length of line in Botetourt County. This pattern confirmed Randolph's 1873 report that a final location in central Botetourt County had not been established. The recorded deeds for right-of-way in Roanoke County covered the total length of line.[30]

Construction was proceeding well. Garrett's annual report indicated that gratifying progress was being made at the heaviest points on the work south of Staunton. This progress was not without problems. By September, the contractor's limit for monthly payments was being exceeded, creating cash flow problems. Garrett had touched on the situation when he noted that 1874 had been a period of great financial trouble with an

Old 199
This B&O Camel Back engine was confiscated by Stonewall Jackson in the spring of 1862 and transported overland by his troops to Staunton. It was returned to the B&O following the Civil War and operated on the Valley Railroad between Harrisonburg and Staunton until 1892, when it was destroyed in a wreck.

Chesapeake Western Railway

extremely adverse effect on new railroad construction due to a lack of available capital. Although he reported the VRR's condition as sound, the depression which had begun in September 1873 was beginning to become evident in its affairs.[31]

By mid-November, the VRR was insolvent. On November 20, the directors were advised that $1,018,068 had been spent between Staunton and Salem and only $270 remained to the credit of the company. The company was also indebted to the B&O for $26,275. The problem was referred to a committee

who recommended suspension of the work by December 1. On the following day, the Mason Syndicate agreed to suspend activities for $40,000. The board accepted the proposal and authorized the committee to make full settlement as soon as possible.[32] The December 1, 1874, suspension of the work between Staunton and Salem would prove to be permanent.

Garrett's optimistic reports of 1873 and 1874 describing the VRR's financial condition as sound were out of touch with reality and misleading to the stockholders. The drastic change in the VRR's financial position between September and November confirmed previous indications that Garrett did not possess the vision, management skills, and leadership qualities needed to guide the VRR during a period of severe economic difficulty.

1875

In February, Garrett resigned. A biographical sketch of his accomplishments as the VRR's president was expressed in the same glowing terms as his annual reports. He was credited with developing the railroad to a high state of efficiency, making it one of the most valuable feeders on the B&O system. History does not support this assessment.[33] Garrett was succeeded by P. P. Pendleton, a B&O vice president.[34]

Activity during the year was limited to operations on the Harrisonburg-Staunton segment. A few deeds for purchase of right-of-way were recorded in Rockbridge and Roanoke Counties.

President Pendleton's report at the fourth annual stockholders' meeting on November 30 indicated that the company was indebted to the B&O for $86,396. The chief engineer's estimate of work completed between Staunton and Salem as of December 1, 1874, was $884,722. Settlement of the Mason Syndicate contract had not been completed.

On the operating section, business results were unsatisfactory and heavy financial losses had been experienced. The VRR

discontinued operations, released employees, and leased the Harrisonburg-Staunton segment to the B&O. The impact of the 1873 Panic in depressing the value of railroad securities was also noted.[35]

During the year the VRR had instituted legal action against Botetourt County to force it to increase the $60,000 previously paid on its $200,000 subscription. In November, the county's supervisors proposed a compromise in an effort to have the action withdrawn. The compromise was based on an immediate $45,000 payment, with payment on the remaining $95,000 beginning when work was resumed in the county. The remaining $30,000 would be delivered on completion of the depot at Buchanan and the construction of a toll-free bridge across the James River at Buchanan. The compromise contract was to be submitted to the VRR's stockholders. If ratified, the county would request the General Assembly to modify the VRR's charter accordingly.[36]

1876

Plans for completing the VRR continued despite the disappointments of 1874 and 1875. The compromise contract proposed by the Botetourt supervisors in 1875 was ratified. On February 10, the VRR's charter was amended to incorporate the terms of the compromise contract with several changes. These allowed the VRR to purchase the existing James River bridge at Buchanan instead of constructing a new toll-free bridge. The existing bridge would be conveyed to Botetourt County. The act also eliminated the depot at Buchanan.

The amended charter also required the VRR to construct a toll-free macadamized road from Fincastle to the closest depot in Botetourt County. This replaced the original charter requirement that Fincastle, the county seat, receive direct service. The preferred location was four miles south of Fincastle, and the macadamized road connecting Fincastle to the nearest depot solved the problem of selecting a location through central Botetourt County. At the same time, it ended the litigation between the VRR and the county. For all its benefits to Botetourt County, the amendment placed a further burden on the VRR's limited financial resources.[37]

The VRR completed the settlement of the Staunton to Salem contract on March 15.[38] With this action, the company had discharged its liabilities under the May 20, 1873, contract with the Mason Syndicate.

The officers continued to seek a way to complete the road to Salem. In November, two proposals were considered. One, from the National Security Iron, Coal and Improvement Company, a Virginia corporation, was to complete the unfinished construction between Staunton and Salem. The second, from the Shenandoah Valley Railroad, was to lease the operating section between Staunton and Salem for $2,000 per month for a period of 15 years.

Both proposals were referred to a committee and to the B&O with instructions to establish terms that would secure "early completion to Lexington or Salem." This was the first indication that the VRR and the

B&O were considering stopping the project at Lexington. The committee rejected the National Security proposal, likely due to the lack of funds. The SVRR proposal was accepted on a temporary basis.[39]

1877

Efforts to develop a plan for resuming construction continued. Early in the year the temporary lease of the Harrisonburg-Staunton segment was terminated because the SVRR had misunderstood the terms of the lease. The SVRR believed that the lease included both the operating section and such further length of line south of Staunton as it might designate. These conditions were not acceptable to the VRR. By the end of the year, the SVRR had removed its rolling stock and discharged its staff. The B&O resumed operations, being reimbursed by the VRR on a mileage basis.[40]

The sixth annual stockholders' meeting was held in Staunton on November 14. The stockholders were advised that $1,200,000 had been invested in the unfinished construction south of Staunton. The estimated cost to complete the road to Salem was $800,000 to $1,000,000, based on using convict labor. The company was also indebted to the B&O for $244,075 which had been advanced to the company to discharge its liabilities to the Mason Syndicate contractors.

The VRR's 1877 report to Virginia's railroad commissioner indicated that $2,536,896 had been spent for engineering, right-of-way, and construction, including the incomplete work south of Staunton. An additional

$3,000,000 was estimated for completion of the work to Salem. Based on this estimate, the use of convict labor offered a significant cost savings.

The use of convict labor on railroad construction projects in western Virginia was not unusual. Convicts were paid 40 cents a day, with the state responsible for the cost of feeding, clothing, housing, security, and medical attention,[41] a practice obviously advantageous to railroad companies.

At the November 14 meeting, a motion was made to resume work by April 14, 1878, and to place a mortgage on the railroad for an amount not to exceed $1,000,000. The motion was defeated, 22,013 shares to 7,071 shares, with the B&O and the city of Baltimore opposed. On the following day, the motion was reconsidered, and authorization for the $1,000,000 mortgage passed. The mortgage bonds were never issued due to the depressed market for railroad construction securities.

While the vote for a $1,000,000 mortgage was reconsidered and passed, no effort was made to reverse the defeat of the proposal to resume work in 1878. The negative vote on resuming work, combined with the debt to the B&O, was an early indication that the local communities had little influence in either the VRR's financial affairs or in a decision to resume work.[42]

The VRR's problems were the least of those facing John W. Garrett and the B&O. In April 1876, the B&O had become involved in another rate war with the Pennsylvania Railroad. It extended into 1877 and impacted B&O revenues so severely that Garrett was forced to cut the wages of the majority of the B&O work force by 10 percent. At the same time, Garrett made an optimistic report on the condition of the railroad to the stockholders and paid the normal 10 percent dividend. This infuriated the B&O workers, and on July 16, they deserted their trains in the Baltimore yards and blocked trains and yards at Martinsburg, West Virginia. In Baltimore, National Guard troops clashed with the workers, resulting in numerous injuries and 10 deaths. The B&O strike spread to other railroad companies with damaging results throughout the nation. The strike lasted until August.[43]

John W. Garrett's cavalier attitude and harsh treatment of the B&O work force may have been reflected in his staff's management and business relationships with the local communities. The B&O considered the VRR a subsidiary, and its larger concerns received first consideration. As a result, the local communities that had founded the railroad and invested in its future continued to experience a diminution of their influence, resulting in a loss of confidence in the B&O's leadership.

The situation was compounded when Michael G. Harman died in Richmond on December 17.[44] Harman had been the leader in organizing the Valley Railroad. Through his personal influence and political contacts in Staunton, Augusta County, and Richmond, he was instrumental in arranging the 1866 and 1867 charter legislation. His leadership brought the local communities and the B&O together, and following the B&O's

and city of Baltimore's financial commitments in 1873, he was an effective spokesman for the local interests in planning, financing, and constructing the railroad. His task had been difficult from the beginning, for there was a longstanding element of mistrust between the local communities and Baltimore interests. Harman recognized early that the VRR could not succeed without the support of the B&O and the city of Baltimore, and he worked diligently to meld the conflicting interests of the two groups. Following his death, no strong local leader emerged to replace Harman and bring together the divergent interests of the two groups.

1878

The year witnessed an escalation of local dissatisfaction with the B&O's leadership and the failure to resume construction.

Prior to the November stockholders' meeting, J. B. Dorman, an attorney representing Rockbridge County, returned from a meeting in Baltimore with the B&O and suggested to the board of supervisors that a petition to the legislature be considered as a means of forcing the B&O to resume work. His suggestion was accepted, and a petition was adopted providing for dissolution of the VRR, revocation of its charter, sale of its property, and distribution of the proceeds. The board requested Botetourt and Roanoke Counties, Lexington, and Staunton to cooperate in the legislative effort.[45]

At the seventh annual stockholders' meeting in Staunton on November 13, William

Keyser, a B&O vice president, was named president pro-tem, replacing P. P. Pendleton,[46] who had died. The stockholders received two propositions. The first was a proposal by the three counties, Lexington and Staunton to divide the assets of the company. The proposition was addressed to the B&O and the city of Baltimore and was presented for the stockholders' consideration. The second was a bid by Mason and Shanahan to complete the work from Staunton to Salem. The bid was rejected.

The proposition to divide the assets of the company specified that the B&O and Baltimore take possession of the Harrisonburg-Staunton operating section, with the local communities taking possession of the unfinished work south of Staunton. In addition, the local communities would receive $214,000 of the bonds held by the B&O as collateral for the VRR's debt.

Keyser responded to the proposition by noting that the B&O had advanced the money which had enabled the VRR to settle with the Mason Syndicate. Further, that although the face value of the county bonds was sufficient to cover the company's indebtedness to the B&O, the Rockbridge County petition made it impossible to sell the bonds at a fair price. Keyser's position was that the B&O had acted in good faith in its business relations with the VRR, but the combined local agitation so impaired the VRR's credit that it was impossible to receive any offer for Rockbridge securities. Keyser did concede that Rockbridge had not failed to make interest payments on the bonds. No action was taken on the proposition and the meeting was adjourned until December 3.[47]

At the adjourned meeting the proposition to divide the assets of the VRR was easily defeated by the B&O and Baltimore. The discussion of the proposal revealed the depth of the mutual distrust which had developed among the local communities, the B&O and Baltimore.

For the B&O, the plan for building the VRR was based on specified financial contributions by the three partners. Keyser critized the local sponsors for failing to meet their $1,200,000 subscription, with only $538,000 in bonds and $30,481 in cash paid in, a total contribution of $568,481. This contribution would be reduced to $354,481 if the $214,000 collateral were returned to the VRR's sponsors. Keyser considered this a one-sided and unfair proposition since $1,018,067 had been invested in the Staunton-Salem construction.

Baltimore was represented by its Finance Committee chairman, Ferdinand Latrobe. His comments were even more critical than Keyser's. He stated that the proposition to divide the company's assets adversely affected the value of all county bonds and that Roanoke and Botetourt Counties had each failed to meet their $200,000 stock subscriptions. Roanoke County had paid in only $25,000, and even this was unavailable because of an injunction. In addition, Roanoke County had not paid for printing its bonds. Finally, Botetourt County had paid in only $105,000. For these contributions, the B&O and city of Baltimore had paid $114,000 for construction in Roanoke County and $121,203 for construction in Botetourt County.

Latrobe reminded the local communities that the 1873 Panic made the sale of mortgage bonds impractical, particularly for an incomplete railroad. The local sponsors were advised to be patient until prosperity returned and allowed the railroad to proceed to completion. In the meantime, the VRR should adopt measures to strengthen its credit and liquidate its debts by making available unpaid subscriptions.[48]

The local communities were unmoved by the B&O and Baltimore criticism. Following December's adjourned meeting, an unsuccessful effort was made to lease the VRR to the C&O.[49]

The VRR's annual report to the railroad commissioner confirmed the position of the B&O and the city of Baltimore. The debt to the B&O had not been reduced and contributions by the local communities were $538,000. The B&O and Baltimore had contributed $2,060,000. With the nation in economic depression, the B&O in a weak financial position with the Baltimore banking community, and with a lack of additional private investment, there was no market for the $3,000,000 mortgage bonds required to complete the railroad to Salem.

1879

The conflict between Rockbridge County, the other local communities, and the B&O continued throughout 1879. William Keyser became the VRR's permanent president during the year[50] but was unable to stem the increasing level of local dissatisfaction with the B&O's management and leadership.

Further indication of local dissatisfaction occurred on January 25 when the Roanoke County board of supervisors rescinded the county's subscription and revoked the authority of Colonel George W. Hansbrough and Henry E. Blair to execute and deliver the county's bonds. Previously, a county citizen, John Trout, whose property would later be crossed by the SVRR, obtained an injunction for the same purpose. The injunction was granted, and Roanoke County withdrew the balance of its $200,000 subscription. Prior to this legal action, only $25,000 of bonds in manuscript form had been delivered to the B&O.[51]

A more farreaching action occurred on April 2 when the Virginia General Assembly passed legislation allowing the counties and towns to revoke their financial subscriptions to the VRR. The legislation, sponsored by Rockbridge County, was based on the petition prepared by J. B. Dorman and the county's supervisors in 1878. It provided for forfeiture of the VRR's charter unless the road was completed to Lexington by April 1, 1881, to Buchanan by April 1, 1882, and to Salem by April 1, 1883. The charter amendment also provided that in the event of forfeiture the whole property of the railroad company would be sold, with the purchaser obligated to complete the road to Lexington within one year, to Buchanan within two years, and to Salem within three years. The counties, towns, and Staunton would succeed to the franchise if the purchaser did not complete the work.[52]

This legislation failed to have the desired result of resuming construction to Salem. In

his report to the stockholders on November 12, Keyser offered a scathing response to the legislation, describing it as a confiscation of the VRR. He noted that the B&O, Baltimore, Staunton, and private investors had paid in their subscriptions, and the funds derived had been used to accomplish significant construction in the counties south of Staunton, while at the same time these counties had not fulfilled their commitments. Keyser noted that the legislation threatened the existence of the VRR by destroying the market for its bonds and making it impossible to obtain mortgages. It created widespread public distrust which adversely affected other Virginia securities. Keyser set forth the position of the VRR's board of directors as having to build a railroad within a specified schedule at the peril of losing its existence, at the same time having the law eliminate the means of obtaining additional financing and investment. Keyser and the directors did not offer a recommendation, other than suggesting that the legislation's sponsors work for its repeal.[53]

The VRR's 1879 report to the state railroad commissioner gave no indication of this turmoil. The financial and statistical data remained unchanged from the 1878 report. A floating debt of $178,254 at six percent interest had been incurred, likely the result of a revenue shortfall on the Harrisonburg-Staunton operating section.

1880

The year witnessed Keyser's efforts to mend the poor relations with the local communities. He experienced some success when the General Assembly rescinded the charter forfeiture legislation of the previous year.[54] On May 8, Keyser advised the Rockbridge supervisors that arrangements, while not complete, were being made to complete the road to Salem.

The VRR's directors issued instructions to resume work south of Staunton and authorized a mortgage to raise the amount necessary to complete the line to Salem.[55] While this was welcome news, Lexington and Rockbridge County remained doubtful that work would resume.

Of the local communities, Lexington and Rockbridge were the largest contributors to the project, having authorized bonds totaling $555,000. They wanted assurance that $210,000 of their unissued bonds would be spent in Rockbridge County, and an injunction was obtained preventing any call on these bonds until work was resumed, with the stipulation that the bonds would be used only for completing the road through the county.[56]

On August 28, the Botetourt County supervisors proposed the award of a $12,087 contract for construction of the bridge over the James River at Buchanan. This bridge had been a part of the compromise contract Botetourt County had negotiated with the VRR in 1875. Although the VRR was required to build the bridge, the county supervisors had decided to proceed independently since there was no prospect that work on the VRR would resume. The county's VRR bonds would finance the work. The

VRR agreed to the proposal, reducing the county's remaining obligation to the VRR to $82,913.[57]

Keyser's optimism for resuming construction was not realized. His annual report, the company's ninth, was presented in November. It informed the stockholders that the prospects of obtaining funds to construct the road south of Staunton were very discouraging and he was unable to advise of any means of obtaining a mortgage. Keyser advised that the VRR would have to depend on its own resources and develop new business opportunities which would increase the company's income.

Even under these adverse conditions, a plan was presented for completing the unfinished construction between Staunton and Lexington. It involved the Richmond and Allegheny Railroad, connecting Richmond to the C&O at Clifton Forge. It was under construction and was located along the James River. It passed through Buchanan and included a branch line along the North (Maury) River into Lexington. A traffic agreement with the Richmond and Allegheny offered the VRR the possibility of obtaining a mortgage which would allow its completion into Lexington, where it would connect to the Richmond and Allegheny branch line. This would allow the VRR to serve the traffic being generated by the mineral resources of the James River Valley and the manufacturing development at Lynchburg. Through its connection to the B&O system, the VRR would then be able to ship the James River ores to the Pittsburgh and Wheeling mills.

A connection to the Richmond and Allegheny also allowed the VRR to extend its service to those parts of Rockbridge and Botetourt Counties located along the Richmond and Allegheny. Although the distance between Lexington and Buchanan using the Richmond and Allegheny route was 17 miles longer than the VRR's planned route between these points, it was over more favorable grades.

Under a traffic agreement with the Richmond and Allegheny, Lexington would become the southern terminus of the VRR, with an extension further south being dependent on improved economic conditions in the nation.[58]

The VRR's report to the railroad commissioner did not mention the extension into Lexington. The value of completed construction was $2,536,896, with an estimated $3,000,000 needed to complete the unfinished 87 miles from Staunton to Salem. The VRR had been able to reduce the balance of the B&O loan to $140,197 by selling county and town bonds held by the B&O as collateral, applying bond interest payments, and from operating revenue.

1881

On January 20, the VRR's directors authorized a $700,000 mortgage, later increased to $1,000,000, to complete the construction between Staunton and the North River near Lexington.[59]

On April 13, the board of directors met at the B&O's Camden Station in Baltimore.

The B&O agreed to take the VRR bonds, not to exceed $1,000,000, discounted 10 percent, and to periodically furnish funds for constructing and equipping the road. The agreement was contingent on the negotiation of a connection contract and traffic agreement with the Richmond and Allegheny. The B&O shared the VRR's view that the Richmond and Allegheny connection was a sound business opportunity justifing the Staunton to Lexington extension. A construction contract with James A. Boyd was authorized.

On the same day, the directors received a proposal from Rockbridge County to convey the VRR south of Lexington to the SVRR.[60] No action was taken. The proposal may have been precipitated by the SVRR's February 28, 1881, decision to extend its road south from Waynesboro.

In July, the directors formally agreed to complete the railroad to Lexington, and efforts to go farther south were abandoned.[61]

The stockholders and directors met on August 11 to consider several proposals. One was a March 28, 1881, communication from the Botetourt County supervisors consenting to the proposed mortgage for the Staunton to Lexington work, provided that the county was released from any obligation to issue bonds for the balance of its $200,000 subscription.

The Botetourt County communication also made reference to negotiations to transfer the VRR between Lexington and Salem to either the SVRR, the Shenandoah Valley Construction Company, or some other company.[62] This may have been related to the earlier Rockbridge County proposal to convey the VRR south of Lexington to the SVRR. Both counties were hoping that the VRR's location through their counties would be used by the SVRR.

The second item of business conducted at the August 11 meeting was an authorization to issue $1,000,000 of first mortgage bonds,[63] secured by the franchise, effects, and assets of the railroad. The deed of trust securing the mortgage provided that the company, with the concurrence of the trustees, could contract for sale or disposition, in whole or in parcels, of the line south of the depot in Lexington. The deed of trust further provided that "if practical to secure the extension south of Lexington by the purchasers of said property, such sale could be made on consideration of the construction of the road, in whole or in part, by others than the Valley Railroad."

This provision failed to attract any buyers for the partially completed work and right-of-way south of Lexington. It marked the effective end of the VRR as originally planned. The high hopes, dreams, and optimism of 1866 for a 113-mile railroad from Harrisonburg to Salem, connecting the B&O system to the Virginia and Tennessee Railroad, were never realized. From a practical standpoint, the end occurred earlier when the Mason Syndicate contract was terminated in December 1874.

On October 6 Boyd was released from the Staunton-Lexington construction contract, which was then renegotiated with

several other firms.[64] On October 15, the Richmond and Allegheny was completed into Lexington.[65]

The tenth annual meeting of the stockholders was held on November 13. Samuel Spencer, a B&O vice president, succeeded William Keyser as president. In his report to the stockholders, Spencer advised that the connection contract and traffic agreement with the Richmond and Allegheny had been executed, and the VRR was ready to proceed with its extension into Lexington. With construction contracts and a mortgage in place, with the B&O agreeing to accept the bonds and advance funds, only the actual construction remained. It would be late October 1883 before work was completed and the first train arrived in Lexington.

Spencer, as Keyser before him, viewed the Lexington extension as an opportunity to increase tonnage and travel on the VRR, justifying its early completion. Spencer noted that the "extension provides the rich ore fields of Virginia an excellent connection to the Pennsylvania furnaces and iron manufacturers where the Virginia ores are very suitable for manufacturing steel. Through the Lexington extension the Valley Railroad can expect large traffic in both directions, iron ores to the north and steel rails and manufactured products going south for equipping southern railroads and other growing industries."[66]

Spencer was the most competent of the VRR's many presidents. He was a Georgia native and an engineering graduate of the University of Georgia and the University of Virginia. He had served the Confederacy with distinction during the Civil War. He was an excellent manager and outstanding engineer. In 1887, he succeeded Robert Garrett as president of the B&O.

Robert Garrett had been named the B&O's president in 1884 following his father's death. He proved to be ineffectual, mainly by continuing John W. Garrett's disastrous fiscal policies. Spencer sought to reform the B&O's accounting procedures and reduce its indebtedness. His efforts proved to be unacceptable to the B&O's directors, and after one year as president, he was replaced. This was unfortunate, for Spencer's reforms offered the B&O an opportunity to correct its financial problems and avoid being placed in receivership, which occurred in March 1896. Spencer later became president of the Southern Railway Company.[67]

EPILOGUE

The cost of completing the Staunton-Lexington segment was $687,201. When combined with the cost of previously completed work, the total construction cost for the 36-mile segment was $997,303, excluding costs for right-of-way and engineering. Only $750,000 of the authorized $1,000,000 mortgage bonds were issued.[68]

One final effort to complete the VRR into the Roanoke Valley occurred on July 11, 1890, when the VRR, the B&O, and the Roanoke and Southern Railway Company agreed to exchange traffic. The agreement noted that the VRR and the B&O were negotiating with various local governments and persons to extend the VRR to Salem and Roanoke and connect to the Roanoke and Southern. The agreement was signed by Charles T. Mayer, president of the VRR and the B&O, and by H. S. Trout, president of the Roanoke and Southern. Trout's signature was witnessed by S. M. Jamison, the road's secretary.[69]

The Roanoke and Southern had been chartered in Virginia and North Carolina in 1886. Construction started at Winston-Salem in 1888 and was completed to Roanoke and connected to the N&W in 1892. Once again Salem had lost an opportunity for a rail connection to the North, primarily because the officers and sponsors of the Roanoke and Southern were Roanoke businessmen.[70]

The agreement could have provided the B&O access to North Carolina and the South, an objective denied it in the 1870s by William Mahone and the Pennsylvania Railroad. Instead, the road was leased to the N&W in 1892 and eventually became the N&W's Winston-Salem Division.[71]

The principal reason for the failure of the VRR was the Panic of 1873. The resulting depression, 1873–1877, severely limited the market for railroad mortgage bonds that were critical to the VRR's capitalization.

The VRR's failure can also be attributed to an accumulation of other factors. While none were as critical as the inability to attract additional capital after 1874, these factors limited the VRR's chances for success. Robert Garrett's failure to negotiate traffic agreements with the C&O and the AM&O, labor conflicts and rate wars that diverted the B&O's attention and resources from the

VRR, and the mistrust generated in the local communities by the failure to resume construction after 1874 were all contributing factors.

Even the 62-mile railroad between Harrisonburg and Lexington was a failure. It was never profitable. The anticipated income from the Richmond and Allegheny connection never developed because the SVRR made an earlier connection in 1882, depriving the VRR of the income from the James River Valley and Lynchburg traffic. The beginning of the end occurred in December 1896, when the VRR's connecting link to the north, the Strasburg and Harrisonburg Railroad, was conveyed to the Southern Railway by the B&O. In 1942 the Harrisonburg-Staunton section was taken over by the Chesapeake and Western Railway,[72] and the Staunton-Lexington section was abandoned and the tracks removed.[73]

The final sad chapter in the Valley Railroad's history occurred on December 29, 1942, when the Chesapeake and Western purchased its entire holdings, including the right-of-way and unfinished construction between Lexington and Salem.[74]

Hungerford's history of the B&O records the Valley Railroad's end as follows: "A little later it reached Lexington, 162 miles from Harpers Ferry. There it halted for all time. Mr. Garrett's [John W.] original plan had been to carry it much further. A right-of-way through Natural Bridge on to Salem had been partly purchased for the extension. At Salem, the B&O would have enjoyed direct connections, not only with the N&W, but with the entire railroad system that stretches itself over the face of the state of Tennessee. Financial difficulties, together with the shrewd machinations of his enemies, thwarted his purpose, however."

Unfortunately, it was the people of Staunton, Lexington, Rockbridge, Botetourt, Salem, and Roanoke County who bore the brunt and disappointment of the VRR's failure. They did not experience the same good fortune as their competitors, the organizers of the SVRR, who were able, under the same financial conditions, to replace their original sponsor, the Pennsylvania Railroad, with E. W. Clark and Company.

Today, their financial sacrifices during difficult times are witnessed by an abandoned railroad, comprised of partially completed excavations, embankments, culverts, and bridges. Dr. E. P. Tompkins offered this conclusion to his history of the Valley Railroad: "Thus passed the railroad which had caused so much talk, so much anxious discussion, so much written in the newspapers and which cost the taxpayers a pretty sum of money. And so the final curtain fell on the tragic-comedy-historical drama of Rockbridge County and its Valley Railroad."

Chapter V
Building the Valley Railroad, Staunton to Salem

THE LEGACY OF THE VALLEY RAILROAD

A legacy is a gift passed from one generation to the next. The gift must be of significant worth and importance so that its history will be preserved and passed on to succeeding generations. Legacies come in many forms and originate from different sources. These gifts can be given by a past civilization, a government, a political movement, parents, an individual, an educational institution, or even a railroad company. The legacy does not have to be a monetary gift; it can be something intangible, a tradition, an education, or something that influences society or makes a mark on history. In all cases, a legacy must have a lasting value that can be bequeathed to a person, to a group of people, or to a community.

For the Shenandoah Valley Railroad, its legacy was to provide the N&W a 238-mile all-rail connection into the industrial North, allowing it to reach its full potential. In turn, the SVRR and the N&W provided the economic foundation on which the city of Roanoke was built. Jointly, they created

employment opportunities and a need for many types of support services that would economically benefit future generations of families, businesses, and industries throughout the Roanoke Valley.

The legacy of the Valley Railroad, an unsuccessful venture that was never completed, is not as apparent. For some, the partially completed and abandoned railroad between Staunton and Salem has little value. For the historian and preservationist, the works that are evident today constitute a legacy, a tribute to the people of Augusta, Rockbridge, Botetourt, and Roanoke Counties who organized the VRR and to the men committed to its building. It reflects their vision, hopes, dreams, indomitable spirit, and financial sacrifice, traits which were necessary if their communities were to recover from the economic devastation of the Civil War. As individuals, their efforts to undertake a daunting task reflect those strong and honorable personal characteristics which are a worthy example for this and future generations. Although they were unsuccessful, their legacy represents an important part of Virginia's heritage.

The VRR's legacy also provides a view into the past. Just as an archaeological investigation of a past civilization reveals the nature and character of its people, their creative abilities and the results of their labor, the remaining evidence of the VRR provides a unique insight into railroad planning, design, and construction practices of the late 19th century.

The extensive expansion of the nation's railroad systems following the Civil War provided the means for the United States to develop its natural resources, grow into an industrial giant, and become today's leader in world affairs. The VRR's remains represent one small example of this national endeavor and reveal the results of the efforts of a unique group of men who planned and started the construction of the VRR from Staunton to Salem.

Although their work was never completed, it was not due to a lack of ability, commitment, or effort. The engineering and construction of the VRR was a significant undertaking. While the construction challenges on the 87 miles between Staunton and Salem were not as complex or as lengthy as many of the railroad construction projects of that period, the engineering and construction tasks were equally challenging to the VRR's engineers and builders.

The 51-mile section between Lexington and Salem provides the best view of 1870s railroad construction practices. Work on this section was started in 1873, suspended in December 1874, and never resumed. The work was stopped at various stages of completion, providing a detailed insight into the construction techniques for building masonry bridges and culverts, making excavations and placing embankments.

The other part of the original 87-mile contract, the 36 miles between Staunton and Lexington, was also suspended in December 1874, but was completed in 1883 under a second contract. Consequently, this section does not provide the same detailed insight into railroad construction procedures as the Lexington-Salem section.

Work completed on the VRR has been dimmed with the passage of time. Its location proved readily adaptable for the construction of today's primary and interstate highways, and much of the work accomplished has been destroyed by highway construction; fortunately, much remains. Excavations and embankments forming the roadbed, masonry bridge abutments ready to receive wrought-iron girders, and masonry bridges and culverts in different stages of completion can be found between Lexington and Salem. In most cases, they are readily accessible by automobile and on foot. These works stand as monuments to the abilities of the men who surveyed and planned the railroad, the men who assumed the financial risk in contracting for its construction and, most importantly, to the men who did the work. The VRR's monuments are one means of recording history for future generations and they warrant preservation by the current generation of historians and civil engineers.

The first step in preparing such a history was the compilation of a record of the remaining traces of the railroad between Lexington and Salem. The second was the preparation of biographical sketches of the engineers, surveyors, contractors, and workmen involved and descriptions of their activities, construction methods, and techniques.

THE REMAINS OF THE VALLEY RAILROAD, LEXINGTON TO SALEM

The preparation of the record of the VRR's remains between Lexington and Salem was based on data contained in the National Archives. The data included a location survey conducted in 1920 by the Bureau of Valuation of the Interstate Commerce Commission (ICC). The survey provided detailed information on the road's location and alignment, the size and location of bridges and culverts, and the quantities of work completed. Based on this data, a field reconnaissance was conducted to determine the VRR's remaining physical features. The results were plotted on United States Geological Survey maps and supplemented with photographs of selected structures and areas of excavation and embankment. These data are included in the appendix.

THE ENGINEERS AND SURVEYORS

Surveys to establish a location for the VRR were started in 1866 by James L. Randolph. Randolph later became chief engineer of the B&O and beginning in March 1872, served in the same capacity for the VRR. As chief engineer, Randolph was responsible for locating, designing, and administering the construction of the railroad. He was born in the District of Columbia around 1817. He was a civil engineer, although a record of his formal education is lacking. In 1870, he was living in Martinsburg, West Virginia, where important yards and facilities on the B&O main line were located. Randolph was often referred to as "major" or "colonel," but there is no evidence of his military service to either the Union or the Confederacy.[1]

Randolph's 1866 survey was a reconnaissance of the 113 miles between Harrisonburg and Salem, likely conducted on horseback. The reconnaissance survey was the initial effort in the overall planning of a railroad. Made without the aid of instruments, its purpose was to establish a general location. In conducting the reconnaissance, Randolph considered a number of factors. The most important was to find a route that would serve the population centers of the sponsoring communities: Staunton, Greenville, Raphine, Fairfield, Lexington, Natural Bridge, Buchanan, Fincastle, and Salem. In addition, the route had to meet specific alignment and gradient controls that would provide maximum operating efficiencies for the VRR's motive power, at the same time providing minimum construction costs. One such control limited the grade of the railroad to 75 feet to the mile.

Charter requirements also had to be observed, the principal condition being that the selected location be central to each county crossed. This requirement, plus the need to provide service to the larger towns, often resulted in a route that did not take maximum

Engineers in Camp

American Railway—Its Construction, Development, Management, and Appliance

advantage of the terrain, thereby requiring steeper grades and greater construction costs.

Following the reconnaissance survey, surveyors were sent into the field to make a survey with instruments, refining the general location and staking a specific line on the ground, measuring its angles, distances, and elevations. In making the location survey, several survey parties were utilized, each assigned a section along the reconnaissance route. Each survey party was staffed with a chief-of-party, a transitman, a note-keeper to record measurements of angles, distances, and topographic features, front and rear chainmen, and a group of axemen and brushcutters to clear a line of sight for the transitman. Following would be the levelman, assisted by two rodmen. Their assignment was to measure the elevation of the line at specific intervals where the terrain was uniform and at abrupt changes in elevation, such as creek crossings, ridge lines, and depressions.[2]

Randolph assigned three survey parties to locate the Staunton to Salem section.[3] These survey parties, designated corps of engineers, were headed by William F. Dandridge, William Jollifee, and Julian Ward. Little is known of Jollifee and Ward but they may have been B&O employees. Their names do not appear in either the 1870 Virginia or West Virginia censuses.

Dandridge was a civil engineer from Winchester. In 1873 he was working for the B&O. In 1875, as a member of the Shanahan branch of the Mason organization, he had a contract to build a section of the Cincinnati and Ohio Railroad in Kentucky. He became a partner in the Mason Syndicate and was later in charge of engineering for succeeding Mason organizations. He retired in 1927.[4]

Each survey party camped at a convenient location along its assigned section. The camp had tents, and in addition to accommodations for the men, there was a kitchen or commissary tent and an office tent, where the results of the day's work were plotted. This ensured that the location being surveyed was feasible and that the data obtained was complete and adequate for Randolph's office staff.

The office engineers reviewed and analyzed the location survey data and determined if any modifications were needed to improve its alignment, grade, and cost. The survey parties then incorporated the office engineers' modifications into their prior survey. If this location proved acceptable to the VRR's officers and directors and to the communities being served, it became the final location for the road and would be the basis on which construction plans were prepared and right-of-way purchased. Where improvements to the location were indicated by the engineering analysis or for local political considerations, further refinements were made by the survey parties until a final location acceptable to all parties was established.[5]

Randolph received a number of directives from the VRR's officers during the course of the survey work.[6] One of the first occurred in November 1871 when he was instructed to have the route from Staunton via Fairfield to Lexington located and ready for contract by March 1872. This schedule was not met, for in March 1872, Randolph was instructed to make a careful survey of a central line through Rockbridge County and, after reporting the results to the president and the Rockbridge County director, was to proceed with a construction contract with the heavy sections on the line designated.

In August 1872, Randolph reported on the status of the surveys: two lines had been located between Salem and Buchanan but they were incomplete; from Buchanan north towards Lexington, about 12 miles had been located; W. F. Dandridge's surveyors were camped eight miles south of Lexington (possibly along Broad Creek near the Broad Creek Associate Reformed Presbyterian Church). They were to meet William Jollifee's group which was surveying 12 miles of line south from Fairfield to Lexington. Julian Ward's survey parties were camped at Midway (2 miles east of Raphine), locating the railroad from Fairfield north towards Staunton.

In September 1872, Randolph was requested to examine the practicality of a route through central Botetourt. Later, he was asked to designate the line and grade for the Staunton to Salem construction for the Mason Syndicate.

In September 1873 Randolph reported to President Robert Garrett that surveyors were revising the route location examined during the summer in order "that not more than one cubic yard than necessary shall be moved" and that some surveys had been made south

of Buchanan "to obtain data from which the company can make a final choice of line."

With construction from Staunton to Salem underway in all counties by September 1873, the incomplete surveys and lack of a final location south of Buchanan account for the minimum amount of construction accomplished in Botetourt County when compared with the work completed in Augusta, Rockbridge, and Roanoke Counties.

The surveys south of Buchanan were eventually completed. The 1920 ICC survey indicates a continuous alignment from Lexington to Salem, suggesting that a final location and design for the 87 miles between Staunton and Salem was established, probably after the charter amendment of 1876 which eliminated the requirement that Fincastle be located on the VRR main line.

THE CONTRACTORS

On May 20, 1873, Randolph contracted with the Mason Syndicate to build the railroad from Staunton to Salem. The Mason group included Claibourne Rice Mason, Edward McMahon, Asher W. Harman, Dennis Shanahan, and Thomas K. Menifee from Staunton and Augusta County, and Joel C. Green from southwestern Virginia. Other participants in the group were two of Mason's sons, Horatio P. and Silas B.

The Mason Syndicate was a railroad construction firm formed by Mason in the early 1850s. Following the outbreak of the Civil War, Mason suspended his construction business and entered the Confederate military.

After the Civil War, the Mason Syndicate completed contracts for repairing wartime damage to the Virginia Central Railroad and the construction of its extension to Covington. Following the Virginia Central's reorganization as the C&O in August 1868, the Mason Syndicate contracted for several sections of its extension from Covington to Huntington, West Virginia.[7]

Mason was one of the extraordinary men of that period. He was born near Troy, New York, about 1810, although some accounts place his birth date as early as 1800. He had no formal education and left home at a very young age. His first experience as a railroad contractor was on a project in Alexandria where he submitted a proposal to complete a specific element of work for a set amount. His proposal was accepted, and using a pick, shovel, and a mule, he successfully completed the work. His first significant project was in 1831, when he constructed a section of the railroad from the Midlothian coal mines in Henrico County to the James River port at Richmond. This railroad required no motive power. Loaded coal cars moved by gravity on a continuous downgrade to the James River. The empty cars were then pulled back to Midlothian by horses and mules.

Other railroads built by Mason were different sections of the Louisa and Orange between 1836 and 1849 and the Virginia Central from Charlottesville into Allegheny County in the 1850s. Mason also served the Louisa and Orange as superintendent of repairs and, following its reorganization as the Virginia Central, was its general superintendent until 1852. In that year, Mason built a

19-mile crossing of the Blue Ridge at Rockfish Gap. This project featured the 1,300-foot Rockfish tunnel, where Mason worked with Claudius Crozet in tunneling under the gap from two directions, at that time considered a daring and unusual engineering feat. This technique was later used in the construction of the transcontinental railroad.[8]

During the construction on the Virginia Central extension, Mason moved his home from Orange County to a large farm, Wheatlands, at Swoope, a small community west of Staunton. In addition to regular farming operations, Wheatlands was used

Claibourne Rice Mason, 1810–1886
Railroad Builder and Founder
of the Mason Syndicate

Doug Kayton, 1998

to winter the horses and mules required for his construction projects.

With the outbreak of the Civil War, Mason, like many Virginians who were opposed to secession, considered the Old Dominion his first allegiance. In 1861 he raised an infantry company, Company H, the Augusta Pioneers, a part of the 52nd Virginia Infantry Regiment. He served as its commanding officer with the rank of captain.

Mason later served as an engineering officer, constructing temporary bridges over the North River and the Shenandoah River at Port Republic in May and June 1862. He bridged the Chickahominy River in the same year, using wagons fastened together with plank decking. In 1864, Mason directed the cutting of a road through the Wilderness to Spotsylvania Courthouse, allowing the Army of Northern Virginia to block Grant's flanking movement.

Mason's most valuable service was in the Confederate Quartermaster Department, where he was responsible for maintaining the railroads in western Virginia. These railroads were critical to the Confederate war effort and were damaged on numerous occasions by Federal forces. Mason and his troops were hard-pressed to keep them operational.

Prior to the Civil War, Mason was a wealthy man. At its conclusion, though destitute, he was able to resume his contracting operations. Two of Mason's most significant and challenging projects after the Civil War were accomplished on the extension of the C&O from Covington to Huntington. One was the Jerry Run fill, containing over 1.5 million yards of material, and the other was the 4,000-foot Lewis Tunnel. These two works, together with the Blue Ridge project, established Mason as one of the nation's outstanding civil engineers and railroad contractors. Mason died in 1886 at Wheatlands. His construction organization, today almost 175 years old, continues as the Mason and Hanger Company, with headquarters in Frankfort, Kentucky.[9]

The VRR's officers and directors had every reason to believe that the Mason Syndicate would complete the railroad from Staunton to Salem, bringing to fruition the dream of a railroad connecting the resources of western Virginia and the Shenandoah Valley to the B&O system, with its connections into the industrial area of western Pennsylvania and the port of Baltimore.

The contract with the Mason Syndicate required that the work be completed in three years, which would have allowed the VRR to begin full operations in late 1876 or early 1877. In Mason and his partners the VRR had contracted with a group of men with extensive railroad construction experience, men who had worked together on previous projects far more difficult than the Staunton to Salem contract. During the Civil War, Mason's command in the Confederate Quartermaster Department included his two sons, Horatio and Silas, Edward McMahon, and J. C. Green. T. K. Menifee and Dennis Shanahan had worked with Mason on the Covington to Huntington extension of the C&O. Asher W. Harman was the only one of the group who had not worked with Mason. He was a successful railroad contractor in his own right and had completed a section of the VRR between Harrisonburg and Staunton.

Mason gave these men the responsibility of completing different sections of the 87-mile contract. Under this arrangement they were side partners, a practice comparable to today's relationship between general contractor and subcontractor. It was Mason's practice to offer side partnerships to men who had demonstrated their contracting abilities and earned his confidence and trust through their performance at the construction site.[10]

The VRR's first construction contract, the Harrisonburg to Staunton section, had been divided into 26 one-mile sections. The Mason Syndicate contract was also divided into one-mile sections, beginning with Section 27 at Staunton, continuing through Section 61 at Lexington and ending with Section 113 at Salem, a total of 87 miles. The contract was divided into six parts. Assignments were:

A. W. Harman, Sections 27–29 and 50–60, three miles in Augusta County beginning at Staunton and 11 miles in Rockbridge County, Fairfield to Lexington.

C. R. Mason, Sections 30–49, 20 miles in Augusta and Rockbridge Counties, ending at Fairfield. This was the only part of the contract for which Mason was directly responsible.

McMahon & Green Co., Sections 61–74, 14 miles in Rockbridge County, beginning at Lexington.

Dennis Shanahan, Sections 75–92, 18 miles in Rockbridge and Botetourt Counties.

H. P. Mason and Brother, Sections 93–99, seven miles in Botetourt County.

T. K. Menifee, Sections 100–113, 14 miles in Botetourt and Roanoke Counties, including the connection to the existing railroad at Salem.[11]

Asher W. Harman was born in Augusta County in 1830. He served in the Confederate army, enlisting at Staunton in April 1861 with the rank of captain. He commanded Company G of the 5th Virginia Infantry, one of the regiments forming the Stonewall Brigade. He later served as quartermaster at Staunton, and in June 1862, was appointed colonel of the 12th Virginia Cavalry. Wounded at Brandy Station and captured near Harpers Ferry in July 1863, Harman was released in early 1865 and paroled in April of that year. Asher Harman was the brother of Michael G. Harman, the VRR's first president. Prior to the Civil War, they operated passenger and freight stage lines. He started his railroad construction business in 1870. Two of his sons, Archer and John, constructed the Guayaquil and Quito Railroad in Ecuador. Asher Harman died in Richmond in April 1895.[12]

The 1928 history prepared for the 100th anniversary of the Mason organization lists the names of Shanahan, McMahon, Green, and Menifee as among the younger men who received their start in the contracting and construction profession from Mason. As noted earlier, McMahon and Green had also served under Mason in the Confederate quartermaster department.

Edward McMahon was born in Ireland sometime between 1818 and 1821. It is not known when he immigrated to America. In 1870, he was living in Staunton with his wife, Julia, and five children. He was a railroad contractor and a partner in the Staunton Iron Works. McMahon attained the rank of major in the Confederate army. In February 1863, he served as chief quartermaster on General Samuel Jones' staff. In December 1863, he was designated chief quartermaster for the Department of Western Virginia and East Tennessee.[13]

Joel C. Green was born in Montgomery County, Maryland, in December 1832. In 1870, he was living in Salem with his wife, Augusta, and three children. Green attained the rank of major in the Confederate army. In December 1863, he served as the quartermaster at Salem. Green was one of the contractors employed on the construction of the SVRR between Waynesboro and Big Lick in 1881. He may have been involved in the construction of the Big Sandy Railroad. Green moved to Wytheville in the 1880s and represented Pulaski, Wythe, Bland, and Giles Counties in the State Senate from 1891 to 1896. He died in Wytheville in January 1900.[14]

Dennis S. Shanahan was a long-time member of the Mason Syndicate and its successor organizations. For the VRR project, his organization was referred to as the Shanahan Branch of the Mason Syndicate. The Shanahan Branch was later involved in the construction of railroads in Kentucky, and he was one of the side partners in the construction of the Chicago Drainage Canal project completed by the Mason organization in 1896. Dennis Shanahan was born in Ireland in 1835 or 1836. The date of his immigration to America

is unknown. Like many of his countrymen, he found employment on railroad construction projects. He was a civil engineer and in 1870 he was living in Allegheny County with his wife, Ann, and four children. One of his sons, Dennis Jr., also worked for the Mason Company on the Chicago Drainage Canal project. In 1869, he was the resident engineer on the construction of the Allegheny section of the C&O, two miles west of Covington. It was through his outstanding work on this project that a difficult tunnel section was completed on schedule. He also served as a contractor on other sections of the C&O extension west from Covington. Shanahan is referred to as "major" in the histories of the Mason organization, but there is no record of service in the Confederate army. In 1878, Shanahan submitted a proposal to complete the Valley Railroad between Staunton and Salem.[15] Due to a lack of funds, his proposal was not accepted.

The H. P. Mason and Brother organization included Horatio Pleasants Mason, Mason's oldest son, and Silas Boxley Mason, his third son. Horatio Mason was born in Orange County, Virginia, on May 7, 1840. He enlisted in Company I, the Orange Rangers, 6th Virginia Cavalry in May 1861. He was later detailed to the Quartermaster Department to assist in maintaining the railroads in western Virginia. He succeeded to the presidency of the Mason and Hanger organization following his father's death in 1886. He died in 1906 at his home near Frankfort, Kentucky.[16]

Silas Mason was born in Virginia around 1848. He worked with his father, displaying a particular aptitude for purchasing, handling, and caring for the mules that were critical to railroad construction in the 1870s. In 1870 S. B. Mason was living in Henrico County and working as a clerk. The histories of the Mason Syndicate and its successor firms indicate that he served in the Confederate army in Thompson's Company of the Light Artillery (John H. Thompson's Battery, the Portsmouth Light Artillery). Following his father's death, he continued to work with the Mason organization, serving as one of the partners on the Chicago Drainage Canal project.[17]

The remaining participant in the VRR contract was Thomas K. Menifee. Menifee was born in 1833 or 1834 in Jefferson County, Virginia (now West Virginia). He lacked a formal education. At age 11, his father died, and Menifee went to work as a cart driver for Humbert and Company, a railroad contractor. By age 16 he had become the superintendent of a Humbert contract on the Virginia Central. In 1858 the Humbert Company sent Menifee to Brazil as the superintendent of its contract to construct the Dom Pedro Railroad. There he was involved in a labor dispute, shooting a man attempting to assassinate the paymaster. A riot ensued, and through the protection of the Brazilian government, Menifee was able to safely leave the country. At the time of the 1860 census, he was living in a hotel in Covington with his occupation listed as "supervising hands on railroad," indicating his participation on the extension of the Virginia Central into Covington, a project completed prior to the Civil War. In 1861, the Confederate military appointed him superintendent of the iron mines in Botetourt County. Following the Civil War, he turned to railroad

construction, working on the Cumberland Valley Railroad in Tennessee and the extension of the C&O from Covington to Huntington. In 1870 his wife, Lucy, and their four children were living in Augusta County. With Edward McMahon, he was a partner in the Staunton Iron Works, and also a director of the Augusta National Bank. Like Mason, Menifee was a self-made man. He died in 1876 at age 42.[18]

Some sources, including family tradition, indicate that the two Gooch brothers were key participants in the Mason Syndicate contract. Stapleton D. Gooch, the oldest, was born in Virginia in 1827. In 1850, Stapleton, a railroad contractor, was living in Hanover County. At this same time Mason was completing the extension of the Louisa and Orange Railroad into Hanover County. Gooch likely had a role in this project and Mason was familiar with his work. In 1860, Stapleton was farming in Louisa County. He was also residing in Louisa County in 1870 with his wife, Molly, and their four children. In 1892, he was one of the partners in the Mason Company's Chicago Drainage Canal project. Gooch's Civil War military service is unclear, but he may have served in the 1st Mississippi Cavalry. Stapleton D. Gooch died in 1902.[19]

Garrett G. Gooch was born in Orange County in 1837 and raised in Louisa County. From 1856 to 1861, he was employed by the Virginia Central. In 1861, he enlisted in the 13th Virginia Infantry, transferring to the Quartermaster Department where he served until October 1861, the same month that Mason was appointed quartermaster in charge of railroad transportation. Following the

Civil War, Garrett Gooch moved to Staunton in 1868, where he married Mary Payne in 1872. His first business venture in Staunton was as a wholesale grocer, later becoming a railroad contractor and builder. He served on Staunton City Council for eight years and was president of a business college, a printing company, and the King's Daughters Hospital. He also served on the Board of Visitors for the Virginia School for the Deaf and Blind and was a director for several banks and the YMCA. By 1880 he had retired from business. Garrett G. Gooch died in Staunton in 1909.[20]

Mason and the Gooch brothers were likely acquainted through their roots in Orange County and their activities on the Louisa and Orange and the Virginia Central Railroads. While neither Gooch brother had any contractual responsibility, they likely played an important role in the VRR's construction.

THE CONSTRUCTION

The VRR's contract with the Mason Syndicate provided for payment of completed units of work at prices established by Chief Engineer Randolph. As part of their total reimbursement, the Mason group agreed to take county bonds at 85 cents in 100 plus accrued interest. The units of work were earth excavation, hauling (embankment construction), excavation of loose rock, excavation of solid rock, culvert masonry, support walls, bridge masonry, ballast, and ties. All prices were by the cubic yard except for ties which were priced individually.[21]

At major stream crossings, the Mason contract was limited to the construction of masonry piers. The fabrication and placing of girders and laying track were not included. This work was accomplished under separate contract, the procedure used in constructing the bridges over the North and Middle Rivers between Harrisonburg and Staunton. These three bridges were built on masonry piers supporting wrought-iron girders fabricated in the B&O's Mount Claire shops in Baltimore. The girders were transported by rail to the bridge site following completion of the roadbed and installation of track. They were then placed on the masonry piers constructed as part of the roadbed contract.[22]

An example of this procedure on the Staunton to Salem section is the crossing of Broad Creek on the McMahon and Green contract in Rockbridge County, where masonry bridge abutments were constructed to later receive wrought-iron girders spanning 45 feet. The method for the crossings of Buffalo Creek in Rockbridge County, the James River and Tinker Creek in Botetourt County, and Carvin Creek and Masons Creek in Roanoke County is not evident. However, approach embankments were partially completed for the crossings of Buffalo, Carvin, and Masons Creeks. At Carvin Creek, stone was delivered to the bridge site, shaped, and dressed before construction was halted in December 1874. Timber bridge trestles may have been used for these stream crossings, although there is no evidence to support this possibility.

With the award of the construction contract on May 20, 1873, the six partners began work concurrently on their assigned sections, and by July work was underway in Roanoke,

Botetourt, and Rockbridge Counties. By September 1, work in Augusta County was underway. Construction methods used by the Mason partners were labor intensive and rudimentary compared to today's methods. Shallow excavation was by pick and shovel, with the excavated material hauled to areas of embankment in wheelbarrows and carts and by horse- or mule-drawn wagons. Ploughs were also used to loosen areas of shallow excavation. For deep excavations, the earth or rock was undermined by pick and shovel and allowed to fall in. Where the length of haul and the quantity of excavated material warranted, lightweight rail tracks were placed on the completed roadbed to move small loaded dump cars to an embankment area.[23]

At smaller stream crossings, arched or rectangular masonry structures were used, with the masonry work being accomplished in advance of placing the embankment. Considerable ingenuity was required of the contractor

Making an Embankment
American Railway—Its Construction, Development, Management, and Appliance

Building a Masonry Arch

Robert S. Fry, 2000

to coordinate the several separate operations in a sequence that would provide the most efficient utilization of his work force.

One of the first operations was the quarrying and conveyance of stone to the drainage structure site. Here it was sized, shaped, and dressed by masons and stone cutters prior to being placed in the structure. Randolph, in one of his reports, indicated that the contractors were able to locate quarries yielding sound stone throughout the length of the project. One was the quarry located south of North Mill Road in Salem. As shown in the appendix, this quarry, now filled in, was located between structures 18 and 19 in the area assigned to T. K. Menifee.

The quarrying operation and the excavation for the roadbed proceeded concurrently, with the locations for placing the excavated material in fill areas controlled by the progress of the work on the drainage structures. Excavation and quarrying in solid rock was the most dangerous task. Pneumatic drills and dynamite had not been developed, and nitroglycerin and other explosives were extremely unstable and dangerous. Drill holes for blasting were accomplished by a two-man team hammering a one- to two-inch octagonal iron bar with chisel end. A black powder charge was placed in the hole, a fuse inserted and ignited. This operation was inexact, for the timing of the fuse burn and the strength of the black powder charge was uncertain. Efforts to improve this operation began in the early 1870s with the introduction of steam-driven drilling machines. These machines were used on the tunnel construction for the extension of the C&O west from

Covington but proved unreliable. It is probable that this type of machine was not used on the Mason contract because rock excavation along the VRR's location was not as severe as the conditions encountered on the C&O project.

The size of a masonry drainage structure was based on the estimated flow carried in the stream crossing. Rectangular or square shapes were used for openings up to six feet in width and semicircular arches for openings up to 20 feet wide. Where larger openings were required for stream crossings, bridges or timber trestles would have been built. One exception was the four-span masonry viaduct over Mill Creek in Augusta County, south of Staunton. It was located on the section assigned to C. R. Mason. This type of structure was likely used to facilitate the transportation of fabricated bridge girders over completed trackwork to the bridge crossings further south.

In a number of instances, drainage structures were located adjacent to the stream being crossed, allowing the work to be accomplished in dry conditions. Following completion, the stream was diverted to pass through the completed work.

For the arch structures, the sidewalls were constructed first, using dressed stone and carried up to the point where the curve of the arch began. The sidewalls were constructed for the entire length of the structure and provided support for timber centering and falsework. Timber falsework was constructed in increments of about 10 feet and provided support for the dressed stone blocks that were placed in courses along the length of the falsework, beginning at the top of the sidewalls and proceeding to the crown of the arch where the keystone was placed. With the placing of the keystone, the timber falsework was removed and then reassembled for the construction of the next increment of the arch. The thickness of the dressed arch ring stones varied from 12 to 20 inches, depending on the span of the arch. This process was repeated until the total length of the culvert was completed. Gin poles, a form of derrick and boom using block and tackle, were placed beside the structure to lift individual dressed and shaped stones into place. For rectangular structures, the same procedures were used, and where the width of culvert opening allowed, a single stone was used to form the top of the culvert.

One of the more interesting features of the project was the 400-foot tunnel described by Randolph in his September 1, 1874, report. The tunnel was located approximately 2,000 feet south of Buffalo Creek (Station 3469) where the terrain rises sharply to an elevation above 1,120 feet in the saddle of a ridge. Only minor preparatory work was accomplished. On the north approach to the tunnel, an embankment was formed from the excavation into the hillside, leaving a nearly vertical stone surface that was probably the tunnel's north portal. To complete the tunnel, Mason would have used either manual means or the steam-driven drilling equipment that he had used in constructing the 4,000-foot C&O Lewis Tunnel. Using this equipment on the VRR's tunnel would have required that the railroad from Staunton across Buffalo Creek be operational to bring the steam engines and drilling equipment forward to the tunnel site. Faced with a contract completion date of three years, Mason would have found it difficult to justify the use of other than manual labor to construct the relatively short 400-foot VRR tunnel.

Within each of the six construction sections, Randolph directed that the heaviest work start first, with the lighter work to follow, in order to complete the entire 87 miles at about the same time or as fast as the track could be laid, ideally from each end of the project. Track would probably have been installed by B&O workers following placement of crossties by the Mason group. As track was laid, bridge construction crews would have followed, similar to the procedure employed on the Harrisonburg-Staunton section.[24]

With work underway in all counties by the fall of 1873, the six contractors proposed to gradually expand their organizations during the winter months, and by spring, each was prepared for maximum effort. This objective was met, for in June 1874, Mason requested that the VRR make payment on each contractor's monthly estimate by the 20th of the following month.[25] By early September 1874, the contractors were advancing the construction at a rate exceeding the VRR's monthly authorization of $60,000,[26] an indication of excellent progress. However, the fact that a limitation had been imposed on the amount of work that could be completed in a given period confirmed that the county bond sales and payments for subscribed stock were lagging, the result of the financial panic of 1873.

By late November 1874, the VRR was without funds and work was suspended on November 25. Randolph was directed to make full settlement with the contractors, based on the value of the work completed by December 1, 1874.[27]

Quantities of each item of work completed, its unit price, and total value were:

Work Item	Quantity (cubic yards)	Unit Price ($)	Value ($)
Excavation of earth	775,448	0.20	151,290
Excavation of loose rock	156,980	0.40	62,792
Excavation of solid rock	385,369	0.90	346,832
Embankment	1,297,797	0.05	64,889
Culvert masonry	17,693	4.00	70,772
Support wall masonry	51	4.00	204
Bridge masonry	17,944	10.00	179,440
Stone delivered and not laid	1,326	3.00	4,158
Cut stone delivered and not laid	869	5.00	4,345
		Total	884,523

The work accomplished by each contractor was:

A. W. Harman, Sections 27–29	$ 25,761	
Sections 50–60	166,740	
Subtotal		$192,501
C. R. Mason, Sections 30–49	$ 192,117	
H. P. Mason & Brother,		
Sections 93–99	12,151	
Subtotal		$204,268
McMahon and Green Company,		
Sections 61–74		$220,641
Dennis Shanahan,		
Sections 75–92		$146,783
T. K. Menifee, Sections 100–113		$120,330
	Total	$884,523[28]

In April 1875, settlement was reached with A.W. Harman, C.R. Mason, H.P. Mason and Brother, and Dennis Shanahan for $137,540 in cash and $74,954 in city of Staunton bonds. Settlements with T. K. Menifee and McMahon and Green were reached in March 1876 for undisclosed amounts.[29]

Suspension and settlement of the Staunton-Salem contract marked the end of the Mason Syndicate's participation in building the VRR. Work on the 87-mile section was never resumed. By June 1875, the Syndicate had obtained contracts to construct 11 miles of the Cincinnati and Southern Railroad in Kentucky, the first step in relocating the firm from its Staunton base to its present-day headquarters in Kentucky. The Mason group also started work in 1875 on the extension of the Richmond and Allegheny Railroad from Buchanan to Clifton Forge. A number of men who worked with Mason on the VRR remained with the firm; in 1892, they included H. P. Mason, S. B. Mason, S. D. Gooch, W. F. Dandridge, and Dennis Shanahan.[30]

THE WORKERS

The importance of the individual worker, skilled or unskilled, in building the VRR cannot be overlooked. His task was difficult, strenuous and dangerous, and was performed in all extremes of weather. Living conditions for the railroad worker and his family were primitive unless his permanent home was located in the vicinity of the project. The abilities and efforts of these men were as necessary and as vital to the success of the project as those of the VRR's officers, engineers, and contractors.

Building the 87 miles of railroad from Staunton to Salem in three years required a large work force. In 1874, 240 men were working on Asher Harman's 11-mile section from Fairfield to Lexington.[31] With this level of employment required for 11 miles of construction, the 63 miles of construction underway during the late summer and early fall of 1874 would have required a total work force of over 1,200 men. Local communities along the VRR's route would have been hard-pressed to supply any significant part of this demand, particularly for the masonry, quarrying, and blasting operations.

The Mason Syndicate contractors therefore needed to recruit large numbers of workers from outside the project area, particularly those experienced and skilled in railroad construction. Unfortunately, time and the size of the work force have obscured their individual identities. Census records for 1870 and 1880 are of little value because the work occurred between 1872 and 1874. Mason Syndicate employment and payroll records no longer exist. Only one man, a stone cutter, can be identified. He was Walker May, an African American and resident of the Kingston community in north Roanoke County, close to the VRR's location. His job was to shape stone for the masonry culverts and bridges. His pay was $1.25 per day.

Although individual workers on the VRR cannot be identified, the demographics of the work force on several canal and railroad construction projects in Virginia between 1830 and 1870 indicate that most of the workers were Irish or African-American.

**Walker May of Roanoke County
A Stonecutter on the Valley Railroad**
Roanoke Times and World-News

The period of great canal construction that occurred in the United States in the first half of the 19th century provides one possible link in identifying the VRR's work force. Canal construction required the same skills as railroad construction. Canal construction involved manual labor, accomplished by men and animals using picks, axes, shovels, mattocks, wheelbarrows, and carts. The work was difficult and dangerous; the men worked from dawn to dusk, with only short breaks for lunch, supper, and a liquor ration. Canal construction required unskilled labor for the most part, but construction of masonry locks, tunnels, aqueducts, and culverts required the more skilled masons, stonecutters, quarrymen, and blasters.

By the 1830s, most canal workers performing unskilled tasks were either of Irish descent or, in the South on projects such as the James River Canal, were slaves of African descent. Neither the Irish nor the slaves worked by choice on the canals; the slave had no choice and the Irishman had extremely limited opportunities to gain other types of employment. Consequently, the Irish moved from job to job. Skilled labor tasks, although not closed to the Irish, were often performed by other workers of European descent.[32]

As railroads gradually replaced canals as a more efficient means of transportation, canal construction slackened, and the Irish turned to railroad construction projects where their canal construction experience was directly applicable. As early as the 1830s, workers on the C&O canal along the Potomac River were moving to railroad construction projects on the B&O.[33]

Prior to the Civil War, Irish workers were employed on the Blue Ridge tunnels and other Virginia Central construction projects. In early 1850, Irish workers from County Connaught working on the railroad near Fishersville in Augusta County were attacked by Irishmen from County Cork working on the Blue Ridge tunnels. Over 200 Corkonians marched through Waynesboro to Fishersville where they attacked the Connaught men and burned the house where they were living. Local authorities were able to suppress any further violence, and a more serious tragedy was averted.[34]

In 1834, 500 Irish workers were employed in building the Winchester and Potomac

Railroad. On the Manassas Gap Railroad, opened to Strasburg in 1854, construction was performed by Irish and slave laborers.[35] In 1870, Irishmen and former slaves were employed on the C&O extension from Covington to Huntington. One of the stonemasons was Harry McKenny, listed in the 1870 census for Bath County as being born in Ireland. On another section of this project, 800 former slaves from central Virginia were employed on the construction of the Great Bend tunnel, located between Alderson and Hinton, West Virginia. Included in this group was the legendary John Henry, a former slave from Louisa County, famous as the man who was victorious in a competition with a steam-driven drill.[36]

These canal and railroad construction projects, spanning a period of 40 years, establish the presence in Virginia of qualified and experienced railroad construction workers. With the completion of the C&O project in early 1873, these men became available for the VRR project and likely provided the largest part of the Mason Syndicate's work force. The master masons were probably Irish, and former slaves performed both skilled and unskilled tasks. Local residents, such as Walker May, represented a smaller part of the work force. Further support for this conclusion is provided by the employment history of the Mason Syndicate after 1874. In June 1875, when the Mason group started work on the Cincinnati and Southern contracts in Kentucky, several groups of workers, including many African Americans, were brought from Virginia. This indicated that Mason wanted to begin his Kentucky contracts with experienced workers, likely those who had been employed on the Valley Railroad.[37]

Convict labor was another potential but less likely source of workers. Convict labor had been used on other railroad construction projects in Virginia, including the C&O extension project.[38] There is no evidence, however, that convicts were used on the VRR's construction, although their use was considered by the directors in 1877 as a possible means of resuming construction on the Staunton-Salem segment.[39]

The vestiges of the Valley Railroad in Augusta, Rockbridge, Botetourt, and Roanoke Counties stand as a reminder of the hardships and sacrifices faced by the Irish immigrant and the freed African American slave in the 19th century. Railroad construction provided one of their first opportunities to build a better way of life. It is appropriate that they be recognized and honored for their individual and collective contributions to the building of America's railroads.

EPILOGUE

The writer's first interest in the Valley Railroad occurred over 50 years ago when his father pointed out a VRR excavation south of Peters Creek Road in Roanoke County, just north of the Roanoke Regional Airport. The excavation has since been obscured by the extension of the north-south runway. Interest was rekindled many years later by newspaper articles describing the efforts of Thomas Fisher in identifying existing VRR structures in Roanoke County.

The purpose of this chapter and the appendix has been to build on Fisher's investigations by documenting the location and remains of the Valley Railroad between Lexington and Salem. It is hoped that this information will create in Augusta, Rockbridge, and Botetourt Counties, and in the Roanoke Valley an interest in preserving the remains of the Valley Railroad.

It is the writer's further hope that the historical societies in these communities will provide the leadership needed to accomplish this objective. A coordinated effort to encourage property owners to grant easements or convey property on which the Valley Railroad was located would ensure the preservation of its remaining embankments, excavations, masonry structures, bridges, depots, and stations.

The preservation of any significant length of the Valley Railroad's remains will create the additional opportunity to incorporate them into the greenways and hiking and biking trails now being developed in the upper Shenandoah Valley and the Roanoke Valley.

Appendix
Valley Railroad Atlas and Photographs
Lexington to Salem

Based on 1920 Survey By
Interstate Commerce Commission (ICC) Bureau of Valuation

Scale - 1 : 24000

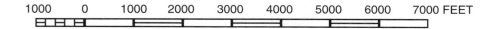

1000   0   1000   2000   3000   4000   5000   6000   7000 FEET

LEGEND

———————   Centerline Construction Not Evident

———————   Existing Embankments—Excavations

—o—   Existing Culverts & Bridges, 4' x 6' and Larger

Existing Smaller Culverts Not Shown

Stations mark the distance along the centerline in 100-foot increments. For example: Station 1425 would be 142,500 feet from Station 0 at Buchanan.

Base Mapping—United States Geological Survey 1 : 24000 Quadrangle Sheets.

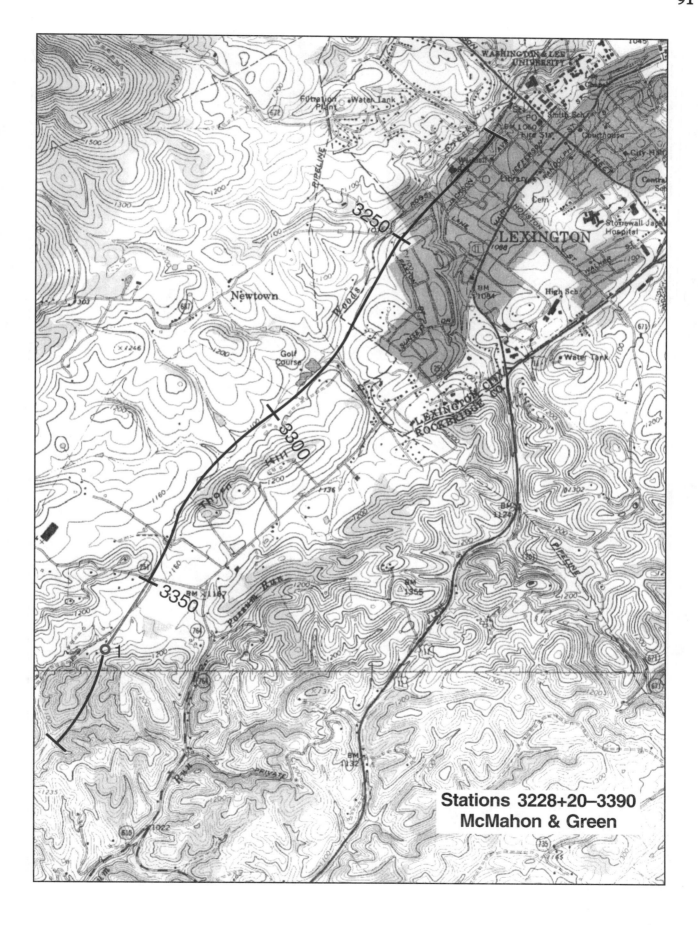

Stations 3228+20–3390
McMahon & Green

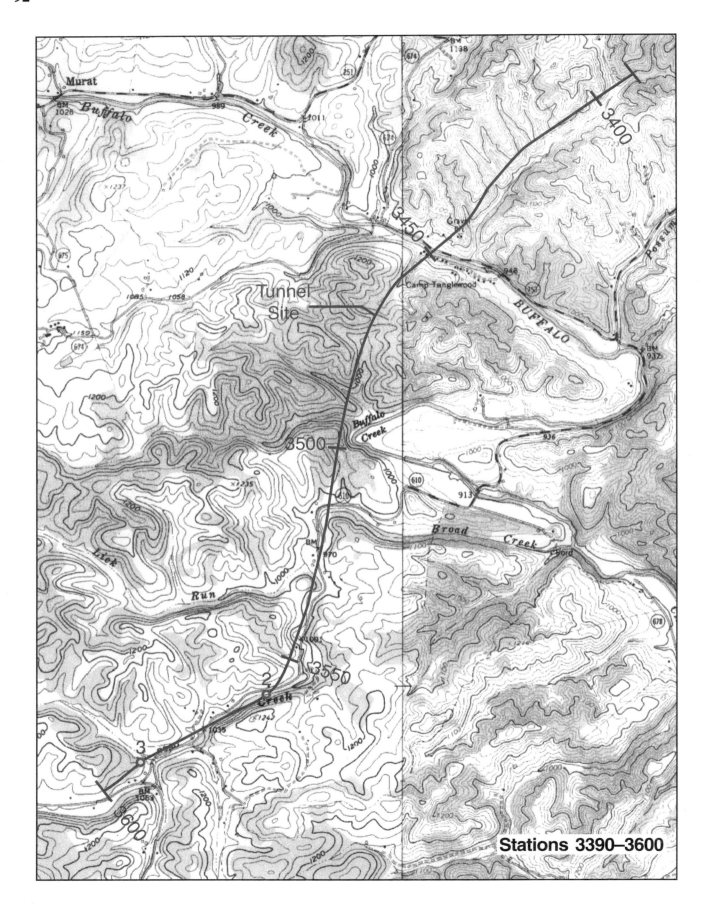

Stations 3390–3600

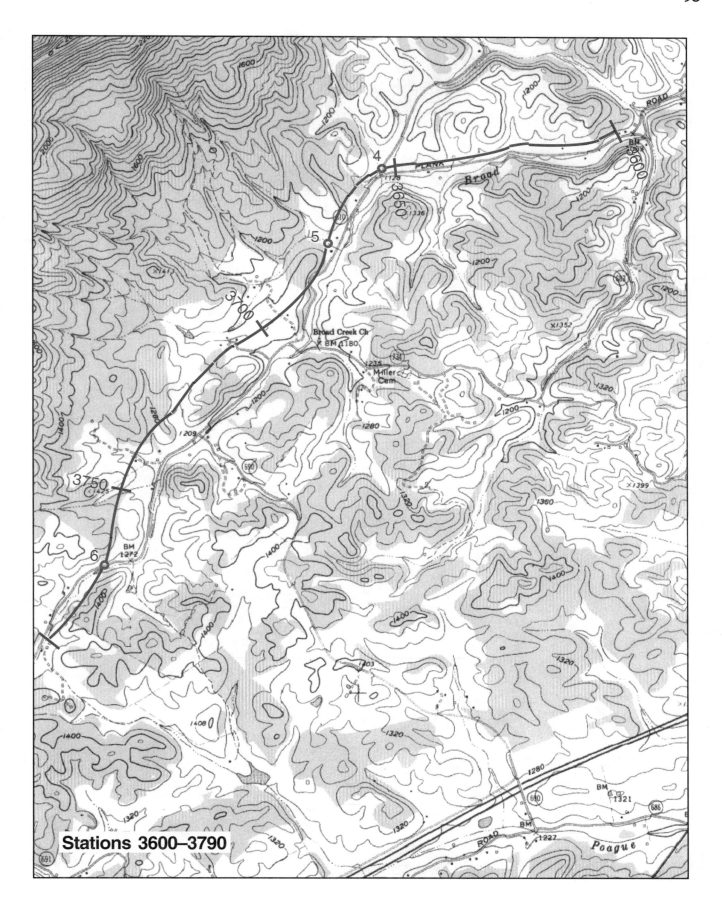

Stations 3600–3790

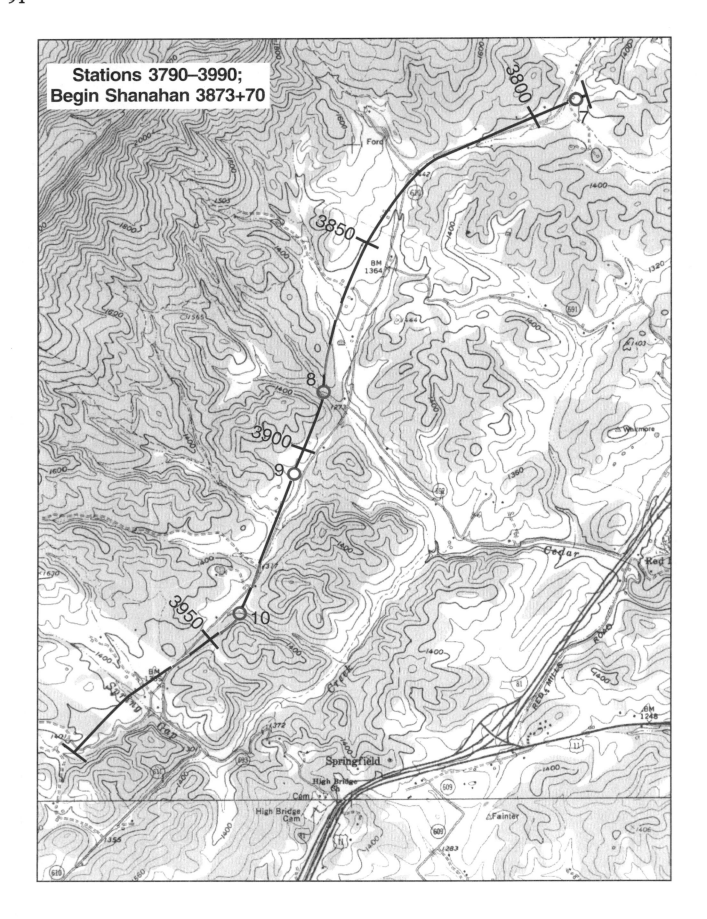

**Stations 3790–3990;
Begin Shanahan 3873+70**

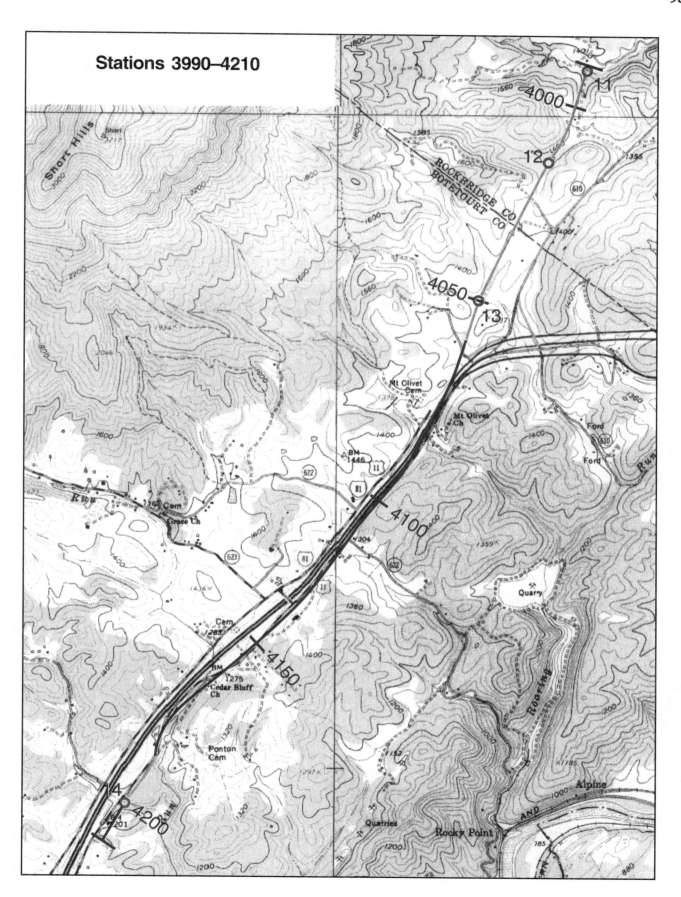

Stations 3990–4210

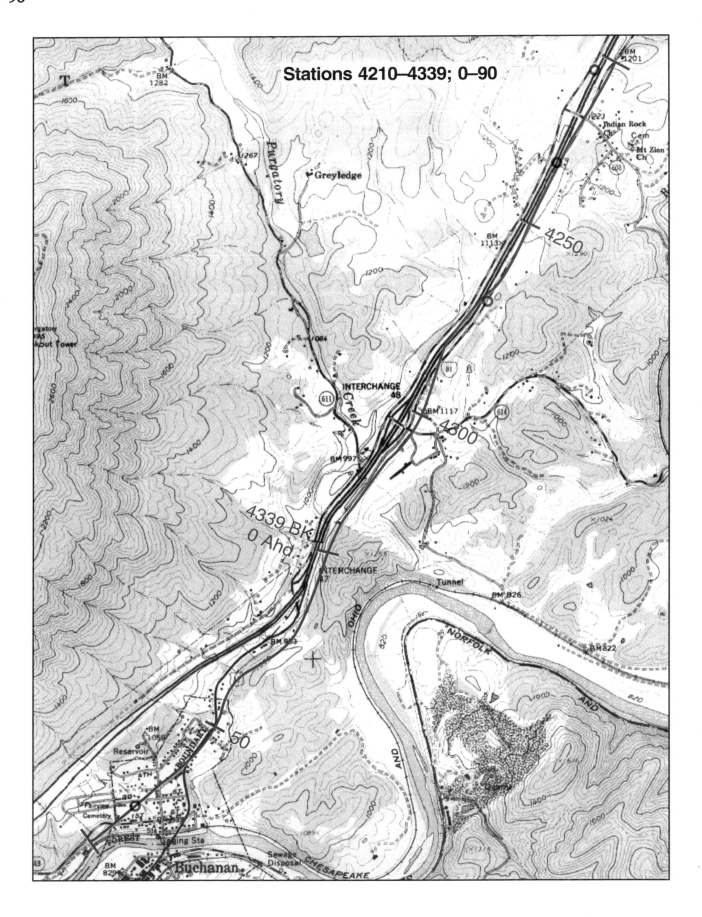

Stations 4210–4339; 0–90

Stations 90-220; 220-380

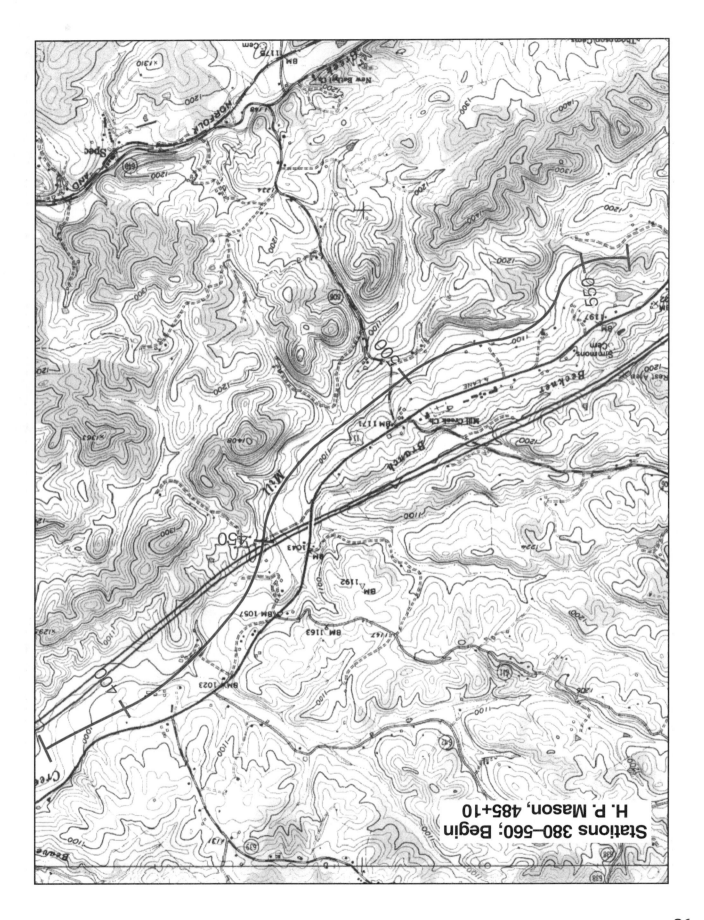

Stations 380–560; Begin
H. P. Mason, 485+10

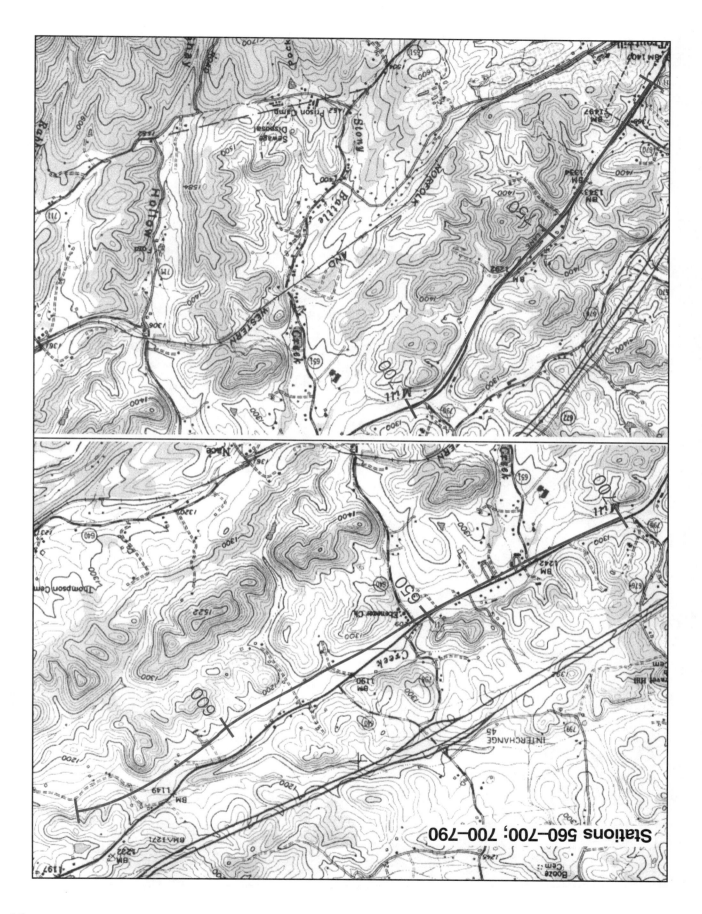

Stations 560-700; 700-790

66

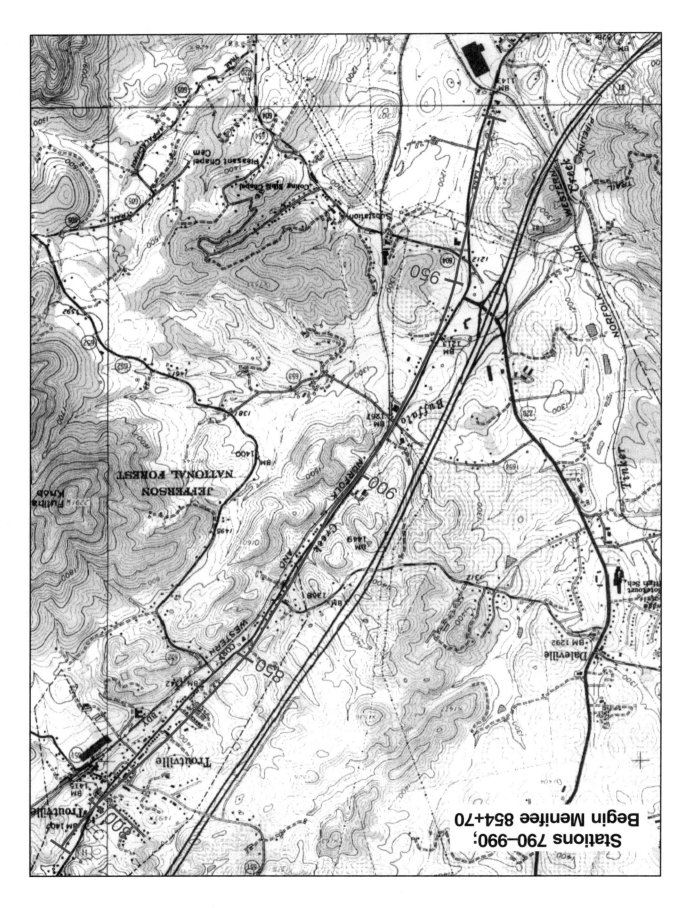

Stations 790–990;
Begin Merifee 854+70

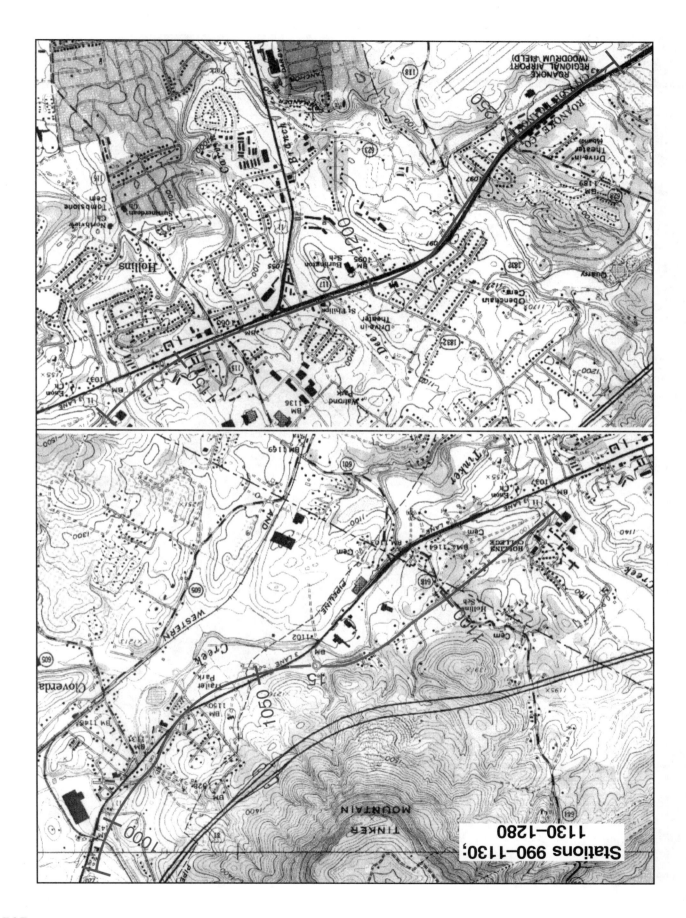

Stations 990-1130;
1130-1280

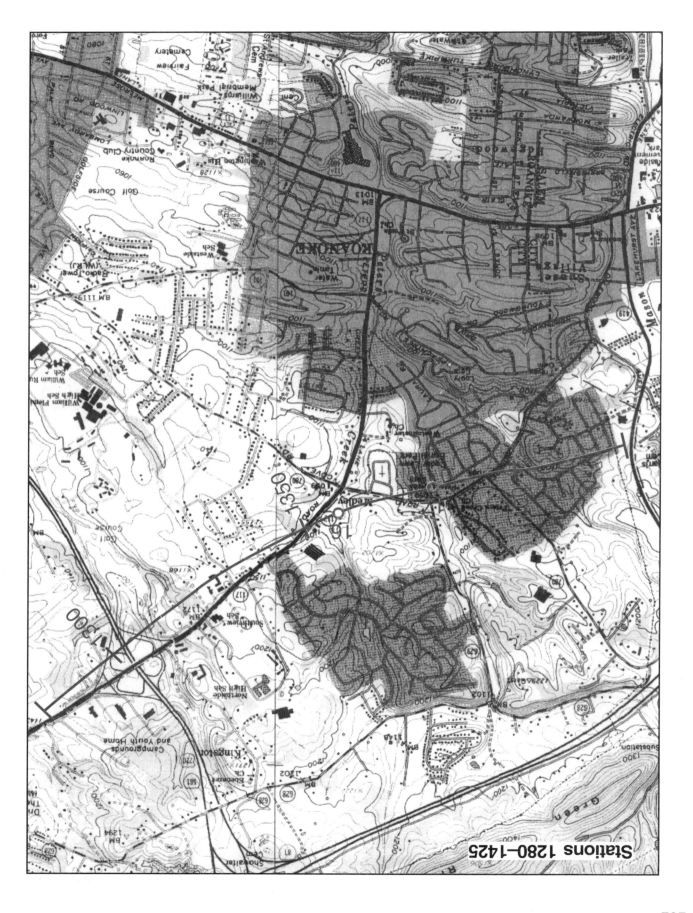

Stations 1280-1425

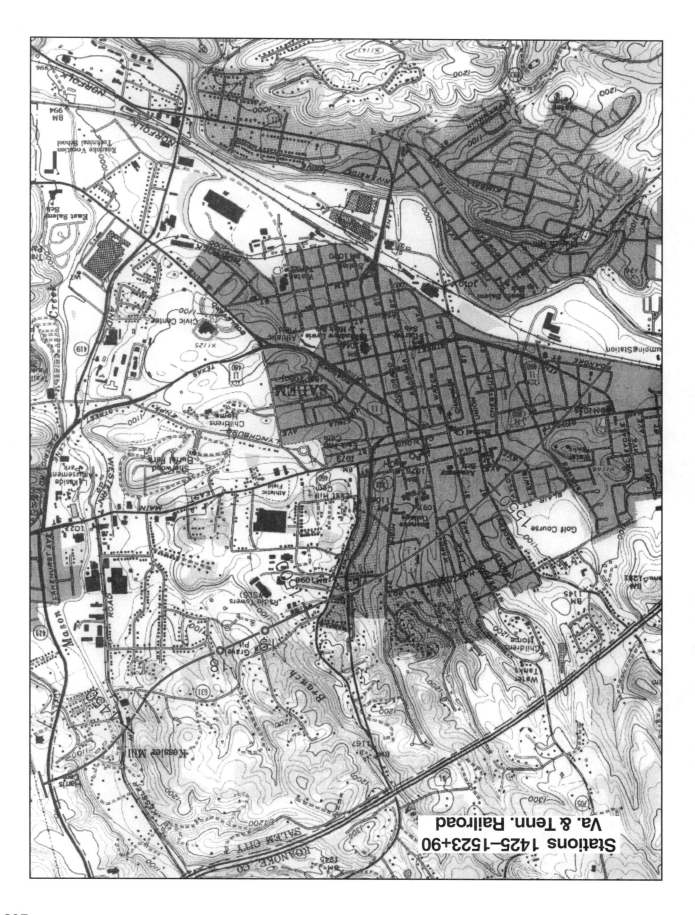

Stations 1425–1523+90
Va. & Tenn. Railroad

REMAINING STRUCTURES
4 feet by 6 feet and larger

Structure	Size and Station	Location
1.	4' x 6' box, 3367+40	On private property on road west of Route 251
2.	Bridge abutments, 3560	Broad Creek, adjacent to Route 610
3.	14-foot arch, 3590+30	Tributary of Broad Creek, adjacent to Route 610
4.	5' x 8' box, 3653+50	Tributary of Broad Creek, adjacent to Route 610
5.	12-foot arch, sidewalls only, 3675+80	Tributary of Broad Creek, on private property
6.	20-foot arch, incomplete, 3770	Broad Creek, adjacent to Route 610
7.	6' x 8' box, incomplete, 3792	On private property near Broad Creek
8.	12-foot arch, incomplete, 3887+25	Tributary of Broad Creek on Jim Shaner property
9.	6' x 6' box, 3907+50	Adjacent to Route 610
10.	4' x 6' box, incomplete, 3942+50	Adjacent to Route 610 on nursery property
11.	20-foot arch, incomplete, 3992	On Howard Link property
12.	8-foot arch, 4013+80	On Haslett property
13.	14-foot arch, 4050	Tributary of Roaring Run on Haslip property
14.	12-foot arch, 4196+60	Tributary of Renick Run, adjacent to Route 11
15.	4' x 6' box, 1065+50	Tributary of Tinker Creek, under Clifftown Road
16.	12-foot arch, 1356+90	Tributary of Peters Creek on Hart property
17.	20-foot arch, sidewalls only, 1381+60	Peters Creek, adjacent to Green Ridge Road
18.	7-foot arch, 1477+50	Tributary of Gish Branch on H. B. Deacon property
19.	15-foot arch, 1488+20	Gish Branch, on WSLC property

Smaller than 4 feet by 6 feet

3' x 4' box, 3358+50
3' x 5' box, 3413+10
3' x 5' box, 3418+03
3' x 5' box, 3428+70
3' x 3' box, 3725+60
3' x 4' box, 3779+50
3' x 5' box, 3897+40
3' x 3' box, 1061+00
3' x 5' box, 1451+60

Roadbed at 3351. West of Route 251

Roadbed at 3510. View toward Lexington

Structure 2—3560. Abutments for 45-foot Bridge over Broad Creek

Structure 3—3590+30. Fourteen-foot Arch on Tributary of Broad Creek

Structure 5—3675+80. Sidewalls for 12-foot Arch. Offset from Tributary of Broad Creek

Structure 6—3770. Incomplete 20-foot Arch on Broad Creek. Upstream End

Structure 6—3770. Incomplete 20-foot Arch on Broad Creek at Route 610

Roadbed between 3770 and 3790. View to East from Route 610

Structure 8—3887+25. Partially Complete 12-foot Arch. On Tributary of Cedar Creek

Structure 11—3992. Partially Complete 20-foot Arch on Tributary of Spring Gap Creek

Structure 12—4013+80. Eight-foot Arch

Structure 13—4050. Fourteen-foot Arch on Tributary of Roaring Run

Roadbed at 4030. View toward Buchanan

Structure 14—4196+60. Twelve-foot Arch on Tributary of Renick Run

Structure 15—1065+50. Four-foot by six-foot Box on Tributary of Tinker Creek

Roadbed at 1080. View toward Troutville

Structure 16—1356+90. Twelve-foot Arch on Tributary of Peters Creek

Structure 17—1381+60. Incomplete 20-foot Arch, Sidewalls Only. Peters Creek

Structure 18—1477+50. Eight-foot Arch on Tributary of Gish Branch

Structure 19—1488+20. Fifteen-foot Arch on Gish Branch

Structure 19—1488+20. Fifteen-foot Arch on Gish Branch

Detail—Structure 19

Embankment at 1510, West Side of Thompson Memorial Drive at Cleveland Avenue

Embankment at 1507, East Side of Thompson Memorial Drive at Cleveland Avenue

Notes

Chapter I

1. Richard B. Morris, Editor, *Encyclopedia of American History* (New York, Harper and Brothers, 1953), p. 431.
2. John F. Stover, *The Railroads of the South, 1865–1900, A Study in Finance and Control* (Chapel Hill, N.C.: The University of North Carolina Press, 1955), p. 108.
3. Allen W. Moger, *Virginia, Bourbonism to Byrd, 1870–1925*, (Charlottesville, Va.: The University Press of Virginia, 1968), pp. 10, 14–18.
4. Stover, p. 66.
5. Stover, pp. 66, 67.
6. Stover, p. 67.
7. Stover, p. 108.
8. Stover, p. 104.
9. Stover, p. 104; Edward Hungerford, *The Story of the Baltimore and Ohio Railroad, 1827–1927* (New York-London, G. P. Putnam's Sons, the Knickerbocker Press), 1928, p. 112.
10. Stover, p. 106.
11. Stover, p. 68.
12. Stover, p. 104.
13. Stover, pp. 103, 104.
14. Festus S. Summers, *The Baltimore and Ohio in the Civil War* (New York: G. P. Putnam's Sons, 1939), pp. 40–42.
15. Stover, p. 105.
16. Stover, p. 118.
17. Valley Railroad Company, "Director's Minute Books, Unnumbered Volume, April 1866–June 1871, Volume I, June 1871–December 1878 and Volume II, November 1879–December 1943," Baltimore, Md., B&O Railroad Museum, Hays T. Watkins Research Library, (Valley, Valley I or Valley II), Valley I, pp. 66, 67.
18. Stover, p. 120.

Chapter III

1. The Virginia General Assembly, "Acts of Assembly, Session 1866–1867," Chapter 237 (Assembly, Session years). Commissioners named to receive stock subscriptions were S. A. Coffman, Henry Forer, and A. M. Newman at Harrisonburg, Rockingham County; Peter B. Borst, William Milnes, Jr., and Benjamin F. Grayson at Luray, Page County; William M. Bock, Robert Turner, and Thomas N. Ashby at Front Royal, Warren County; Loyd Logan, Henry M. Brent, and Philip Williams at Winchester, Frederick County; David H. McGwin, William N. Nelson, and David Meade at Berryville, Clarke County; Nicholas K. Trout, Michael G. Harman and George Baylor at Staunton, Augusta County; James S. Paxton, John McD.

Taylor, and William C. Lewis at Lexington, Rockbridge County; John S. Wilson, William D. Couch, and Alphonso Finney at Buchanan, Botetourt County; W. E. M. Word, T. G. Goodwin, and W. A. Glasgow at Fincastle, Botetourt County; Bernard Pitzer, Frederick Johnston, and George W. Shanks at Salem, Roanoke County; John B. White, George J. Stevens, Wyatt S. Beasley, James F. Affield and William T. Sims at Stanardsville, Greene County.
2. Assembly, Session 1869–1870, Chapter 42.
3. Shenandoah Valley Railroad Company, "Stockholders' and Directors' Minute Book A, 1870–1881 and Minute Book B, 1881–1887," (Shenandoah Valley A or B), Special Collections Department of the University Libraries of Virginia Tech. Shenandoah Valley A, p. 32.
4. Assembly, Session 1869–1870, Chapter 197.
5. 1870 Census, Page County, Va.; Harry M. Strickler, *A Short History of Page County, Virginia* (Harrisonburg, Va.: C. J. Carrier, 1974, c. 1952), pp. 377, 382.
6. Shenandoah Valley A, p. 1.
7. Shenandoah Valley A, p. 7.
8. Paul J. Westhaffer, *History of the Cumberland Valley Railroad, 1835–1919* (Washington, D.C. Chapter, National Railway Historical Society, 1979), p. 133.
9. Shenandoah Valley A, p.7.
10. Millard A. Bushong, *A History of Jefferson County, West Virginia*, (Charles Town, W.Va.: Jefferson Publishing Company), 1941, pp. 218, 233; Stuart E. Brown, Jr., *Annals of Clarke County* (Berryville, Va.: Virginia Book Company, 1983), p. 152; Strickler, p. 204.
11. Bushong, p. 233.
12. Shenandoah Valley A, p. 16.
13. Robert L. Frey, Editor, *Encyclopedia of American Business History and Biography, Railroads in the Nineteenth Century*, New York and Oxford, Facts on File, A Bruccoli, Clark, Layman Book, 1988, p. 358.
14. John F. Stover, *The Railroads of the South, 1865–1900, A Study in Finance and Control* (Chapel Hill: The University of North Carolina Press), pp. 104, 105.
15. Allen W. Moger, *Virginia, Bourbonism to Byrd, 1870–1925* (Charlottesville: The University Press of Virginia), p.18.
16. Stover, p. 110.
17. Stover, p. 118.
18. Frey, p. 361.
19. Shenandoah Valley A, p. 51.
20. Shenandoah Valley A, p. 63.
21. Shenandoah Valley A, p. 77.
22. Shenandoah Valley A, p. 87.
23. Shenandoah Valley A, p. 93.

24. Richard K. MacMaster, *Augusta County History 1865–1950* (Staunton, Va.: Augusta County Historical Society, 1987), p. 68.
25. Stover, p. 127.
26. Shenandoah Valley A, pp. 115–17.
27. Westhaffer, p. 138.
28. Shenandoah Valley A, p. 121.
29. Shenandoah Valley A, p. 120.
30. Shenandoah Valley A, p. 127.
31. The Virginia General Assembly, "Acts and Joint Resolutions passed by the General Assembly of the State of Virginia, Session 1872–1873," Chapter 113 (Assembly, Session years).
32. Frey, pp. 61–63.
33. Frey, pp. 314, 361; Stover, pp. 119, 120.
34. Shenandoah Valley A., p. 130.
35. Shenandoah Valley A., p. 133. Milnes' report that the Central Improvement Company contract would be considered void unless it resumed work immediately would later be the basis for a stockholder's objection to the financial settlement ultimately negotiated with Central Improvement in 1880.
36. Shenandoah Valley A, p. 134.
37. Stover, p. 138.
38. Shenandoah Valley A, p. 140.
39. Shenandoah Valley A, p. 145.
40. Shenandoah Valley A, p. 147.
41. Shenandoah Valley A, p. 154.
42. Strickler, p. 224.
43. Shenandoah Valley A, p. 155.
44. Brown, pp. 151, 152.
45. Shenandoah Valley A, p. 156.
46. Shenandoah Valley A, pp. 157–59.
47. Stover, p. 138.
48. Shenandoah Valley A, pp. 160, 161.
49. Shenandoah Valley A, pp. 163, 164. The full text of Milnes' report to the stockholders on negotiations with the Valley Railroad is as follows. "With a view of the furtherance of the interest of this Company by securing, at a future day, a practical connection at Harrisonburg with the Valley Railroad, the President and Directors of this Road, at the commencement of the past year, obtained upon the terms of a written proposition from the President and Directors of the Valley Railroad a temporary lease of the completed line of 26 miles from Harrisonburg to Staunton, with a distinct understanding and agreement that the said lease should be extended to such further length of line, not exceeding 15 years, as might be desired by the Shenandoah Valley Railroad Company. On these conditions and under these expectations the Shenandoah Valley Railroad took possession of the Valley Railroad between the points indicated, procured all the necessary rolling stock and appointed all the necessary agents for the operation of the road thus passing into their hands. The President and Directors however, regret to be compelled to say that the hopes held out to them by an extension of their said lease have been frustrated by the refusal of the Valley Railroad to comply with the terms of the proposition under which the temporary lease was in fact affected, and having thus failed in the accomplishment of the purposes of the original agreement, the President and Directors of this Company gave the necessary notice for the termination of the arrangement entered into, and surrendered at the end of six months the Valley Road to its proper authorities, withdrew its rolling stock, discharged the agents employed and paid off all the liabilities incurred in its management."
50. Shenandoah Valley A, p. 164.
51. Shenandoah Valley A, p. 167.
52. Shenandoah Valley A, p. 168.
53. Brown, p.152.
54. Shenandoah Valley A, p. 168.
55. Shenandoah Valley A, pp. 172, 175. The basis of the opposition to the re-election of Milnes as president is unknown but may have been founded in the long delay in resuming construction.
56. Shenandoah Valley A, p. 181. William H. Travers of Jefferson County, W.Va., one of the first directors, was named trustee of the original 1872 mortgage, replacing J. Edgar Thomson, president of the Pennsylvania, and his successor as trustee, Matthew Baird, both of whom had died.
57. Shenandoah Valley A, p. 183.
58. Shenandoah Valley A, p. 185.
59. Westhaffer, p.135.
60. Shenandoah Valley A, p. 185.
61. E. F. Striplin, *The Norfolk and Western, A History* (The Norfolk and Western Railway Company, 1981), p. 66.
62. Shenandoah Valley A, p. 192.
63. Mason Y. Cooper, *Norfolk and Western's Shenandoah Valley Line* (Norfolk and Western Historical Society, Inc., 1998), pp. 10, 17.
64. Striplin, pp. 60, 71.
65. Striplin, p. 71.
66. Striplin, pp. 61, 65; Frey, p. 58; Cooper, p. 18.
67. Shenandoah Valley A, p. 200.
68. Shenandoah Valley A, p. 203.
69. Strickler, p. 196.
70. Cooper, p. 22.
71. Shenandoah Valley A, pp. 206–9.
72. Cooper, p. 22.
73. Shenandoah Valley A, p. 208; Roanoke County Clerk of the Circuit Court, Deed Book L, p. 464.
74. Shenandoah Valley A, p. 211.
75. Westhaffer, p. 20.
76. MacMaster, p.68.
77. Shenandoah Valley A, p. 222.
78. Shenandoah Valley A, p. 237.
79. Cooper, p. 23.
80. Cooper, p. 242; Strickler, pp. 204, 205.
81. "Corporate History, Shenandoah Valley Railway Company; Maryland and Washington Division of the Norfolk and Western Railroad, 1891, p. 4. (Corporate History, SVRCo.); Brown, p. 286; J. Thomas Scharf, "History of Western Maryland, being a history of Frederick, Montgomery, Carroll, Washington, Allegheny, and Garrett Counties," (Baltimore Regional Publishing Company, 1968), p. 1016.
82. Striplin, p. 61.
83. Allen W. Moger, "Railroad Practices and Policies," *Virginia Magazine of History and Biography*, October 1951, p. 434.
84. Shenandoah Valley A, p. 244.
85. Corporate History, SVRCo., p. 4.
86. Shenandoah Valley A, p. 248.
87. Shenandoah Valley A, pp. 250–94.
88. Shenandoah Valley A, pp. 295–98. The 238-mile length of the Shenandoah Valley reported by Kimball was a 5-mile reduction in the length required by the original plan to connect at Salem.
89. Norwood C. Middleton, *Salem, A Virginia Chronicle* (Salem, Va.: Salem Historical Society, Inc., 1986), pp. 124–27.
90. Raymond P. Barnes, *A History of Roanoke* (Radford, Va.: Commonwealth Press Inc., 1968), p. 87.
91. Workers of the Writer's Program of the Works Project Administration in the State of Virginia, "Roanoke, Story of City and County," American Guide Series, 1942, (WPA VA) p. 191.
92. Clare White, *Roanoke 1740–1982* (Roanoke Valley Historical Society, 1982), p. 63. Participants in the meeting may have included M. C. Thomas, P. L. Terry, who later became a director of the Roanoke Machine Works, Ferdinand Rorer, J. M. Gambill, Henry S. Trout, John Kefauver, George P. Tayloe, W. H. Startzman, James Neal, C. W. Thomas, who delivered the Big Lick subscription to John C. Moomaw, T. T. Fishburne, S. W. Jamison, C. M. Turner, and M. Waid.

93. Couper, "History of the Shenandoah Valley," p. 1034.
94. Shenandoah Valley B, pp. 4, 5.
95. White, p. 63.
96. MacMaster, p. 68.
97. Strickler, p. 205.
98. Roanoke County Clerk of the Circuit Court, Charter Book 1, p. 25.
99. Shenandoah Valley B, p. 62.
100. Shenandoah Valley B, pp. 27, 28.
101. Shenandoah Valley B, p. 66.
102. Shenandoah Valley B, pp. 46–60.
103. Shenandoah Valley B, pp. 74–77.
104. Corporate History, Shenandoah Valley Railway Co., p. 4. The engineer of the first train into Big Lick was Stephen Lacy Mayo, of Ivy, Virginia, a former University of Virginia student. His lifelong ambition had been to be a locomotive engineer, which he realized with the Shenandoah Valley Railroad. Attributed to Mary Francis Fisher Boone, a descendent.
105. Strickler, p. 198.

Chapter IV

1. The Virginia General Assembly, "Acts of Assembly, Session 1866–1867," Chapter 207 (Assembly, Session years). The commissioners named to receive stock subscriptions were A. M. Newman, S. A. Coffman and M. Harvey Effinger at Harrisonburg, Rockbridge County; Nicholas K. Trout, Michael G. Harman, and George Baylor at Staunton, Augusta County; James G. Paxton, Dr. James McD. Taylor, and William C. Lewis at Lexington, Rockbridge County; John S. Wilson, William D. Couch, and Alphonzo Finney at Buchanan, Botetourt County; William E. M. Word, Thomas G. Godwin, and William A. Glasgow at Fincastle, Botetourt County; Bernard Pitzer, Frederick Johnston, and George W. Shanks at Salem, Roanoke County.
2. Raymond P. Barnes, *A History of Roanoke* (Radford, Va.: Commonwealth Press Inc., 1968), p. 67; J. W. Wayland, "A History of Rockingham County," Dayton, Va., 1912, p. 228; Matthew W. Paxton, Jr., "Bringing the Railroad to Lexington, 1866–1883," Rockbridge Historical Society Proceeding X (1980–1989), p. 182; Richard K. MacMaster, "Augusta County History, 1865–1950," Augusta County Historical Society, 1987, p. 64; Valley Railroad Company, "Director's Minute Books, Unnumbered Volume, April 1866–June 1871, Volume I, June 1871–December 1878 and Volume II, November 1879–December 1943," B&O Railroad Museum, The Hays T. Watkins Research Library, Baltimore, Md. (Valley, Valley I or Valley II), Valley, p.7. Directors elected at the organizing convention were W. E. M. Word, Fincastle; Edmund Pendleton, Botetourt County; James T. Patton, Fairfield; C. D. E. Brady (or Bradley), Buffalo Forge; Dr. J. B. Strayer, New Market; M. Harvey Effinger and Dr. S. A. Coffman, Rockingham County; and John Echols, Bolivar Christian, and William Allan, Augusta County.
3. MacMaster, p. 62; Robert Driver, *52nd Virginia Infantry* (Lynchburg, Va.: H. E. Howard Inc., 1986), p. 118; Thomas S. Harman, "The Secession Crisis in the Shenandoah Valley, How Staunch Unionists Became Ardent Confederates," p. 46.
4. MacMaster, p. 64; Valley, p. 10; J. Randolph Kean, *The Development of the 'Valley Line' of the Baltimore and Ohio Railroad* (*Virginia Magazine of History and Biography*, October, 1952), p. 545; Valley, p. 10.
5. Assembly, Session 1866–1867, Chapter 284.
6. Valley, pp. 12, 27.
7. Kean, pp. 544–47; John F. Stover, *The Railroads of the South, 1865–1900, A Study in Finance and Control* (Chapel Hill: The University of North Carolina Press, p.1868).
8. Barnes, pp. 67, 69; Valley, p. 34. One of Robert E. Lee's first actions as VRR president was an August 30, 1870, invitation to the Roanoke County Board of Supervisors to participate in the company's financing, promising equal representation with Botetourt County on the board of directors.
9. Paxton, p. 182; Dr. E. P. Tompkins, *The Valley Railroad* (Rockbridge Historical Society Collection, Washington and Lee University, 1947), p. 19; Allen W. Moger, *Railroad Practices and Policies* (*Virginia Magazine of History and Biography*, October, 1951), p. 450, (Moger 1).
10. MacMaster, p. 66.
11. Paxton, p. 183.
12. Kean, p. 547; Valley I, p. 29.
13. D. S. Freeman, *Robert E. Lee, A Biography, Volume IV* (New York: Charles Scribner's Sons, 1948), p. 480.
14. Valley I, p. 76; General Lee's July 28, 1870, letter was written from Washington College, Lexington and was addressed to M. G. Harman, President, Colonel John B. Baldwin, Judge Hugh Sheffey, Honorable A. H. H. Stuart, Thomas I. Michie, Esquire, and others. It read as follows: "Your favor of July 25 has been received. In response to your kindness in urging me to accept the presidency of the Valley Railroad and to your request that, if agreeable, I should signify my willingness to do so, I have to say that I have no desire for the office and would much prefer that it should be conferred to some other gentleman, yet so important do I regard this work to the interest of the Valley and of the whole state, that when the company is fully organized, if the desire of my services as president and think proper to make such arrangements as may render my acceptance of the position not incompatible with my present duties, I shall be willing to accept the control of the road and to use what energy and ability I may possess in furthering the speedy completion of the work."
15. Allen W. Moger, *Virginia, Bourbonism to Byrd, 1870–1925* (Charlottesville: The University Press of Virginia), pp. 5–7 (Moger 2).
16. "History of Washington and Lee, Heritage," 1995, Washington and Lee University Web page.
17. *Virginia Magazine of History and Biography*, Vol. 4, No. 4, April 1897, "Necrology, Robert Garrett," p. 458, (Biography, Robert Garrett).
18. Kean, p.547; Valley I, pp. 51, 52, 54.
19. Robert Garrett, "First Valley Railroad Company Report to the Board of Public Works," Staunton, Virginia, October 30, 1872 (Garrett 1); Valley I, p. 92.
20. Valley I, pp. 60, 61, 65–67, 92.
21. Valley I, pp. 69, 70, 71.
22. Robert Garrett, "Second Valley Railroad Company Report to the Board of Public Works, 1872–1873," pp. 152–55 (Garrett 2).
23. Garrett 2, pp. 156, 157.
24. Garrett 2, p. 153.
25. Stover, p. 127.
26. Tompkins, p.6.
27. Garrett 2, p. 155; Kean, p. 547; Barnes, p. 69; Valley I, pp. 29, 33.
28. Garrett 2, p. 157.
29. Paxton, p. 184.
30. Grantee Records, Offices of the Clerk of the Circuit Court, Rockbridge, Botetourt, and Roanoke Counties.
31. Valley I, p. 135.
32. Valley I, p. 140.
33. Biography Robert Garrett, p. 458.
34. Tompkins, p. 22.
35. Valley I, pp. 194, 195, 217, 218.
36. Valley I, p. 230.
37. The General Assembly of Virginia, "Acts and Joint Resolutions Passed by the General Assembly of the State of Virginia, Session 1875–1876," Chapter 5 (Assembly, Session years).
38. Valley I, p. 258.
39. Valley I, p. 336; Shenandoah Valley Railroad Company, "Stockholders' and Directors' Minutes, Book A, 1870–1881 and Book B, 1881–1887,"

(Shenandoah Valley A or B), Special Collections Department of the Universities at Virginia Tech. Shenandoah Valley A, p. 15.

40. Shenandoah Valley A, p. 164.
41. Moger 1, pp. 451, 452.
42. Valley I, pp. 368–67.
43. Frey, p. 137.
44. MacMaster, p. 67; Driver, p. 118.
45. Tompkins, pp. 20, 21; Paxton, pp. 185, 186.
46. Valley I, p. 395.
47. Valley I, p. 398.
48. Valley I, pp. 408–16.
49. Paxton, p. 185.
50. Valley II, p. 3.
51. Valley I, p. 416; Barnes, p. 70.
52. Assembly, Session 1878–1879, Chapter 74.
53. Valley II, p. 3.
54. Assembly, Session 1879–1880, Chapter 173.
55. Tompkins (manuscript), p. 9.
56. Tompkins, pp. 21, 22.
57. Valley II, p. 37.
58. Valley II, p. 25.
59. Valley II, p. 63.
60. Valley II, pp. 63, 44.
61. Valley II, pp. 46–48.
62. Valley II, pp. 50, 51.
63. Clerk's Office of the Circuit Court of Roanoke County, Deed Book M, p.194.
64. Valley II, p. 49.
65. Paxton, p. 186.
66. Valley II, p. 63.
67. Burke Davis, *The Southern Railway, Road of the Innovators* (Chapel Hill and London: The University of North Carolina Press, 1985), pp. 19, 20, 24, 25; John Moody, *The Railroad Builders, A Chronicle of the Welding of the States* (New York: United States Publishers Association, 1919), pp. 108, 109; Frey, p. 22.
68. Annual Report of the Railroad Commissioner to the General Assembly of Virginia, "Valley Railroad Company Report, 1884."
69. Roanoke Chapter, National Railway Historical Society, "Agreement, B&O Railroad Company, Valley Railroad Company, and Roanoke and Southern Railway Company, July 11, 1890."
70. Barnes, pp. 163–65.
71. Barnes, p. 165.
72. Kean, p. 550.
73. Paxton, p. 190.
74. Clerk's Office of the Circuit Court of Roanoke County, Deed Book 302, p. 45.

Chapter V

1. Richard K. MacMaster, "Augusta County History, 1865–1950," Staunton, Va., Augusta County Historical Society, 1987, p. 64; Valley Railroad Company, "Director's Minute Book, Volume I, June 1871–December 1878, and Volume II, November 1879–December 1943," (Valley I and Valley II), Baltimore, Maryland, B&O Railroad Museum, The Hays T. Watkins Research Library, Valley I, p.65; 1870 Census, New York.
2. Thomas M. Cooley, *American Railway—Its Construction, Development, Management and Appliance* (New York: Charles Scribner's Sons, 1889), pp. 13–15.
3. Valley I, pp. 69, 70.
4. Ann Arnold Lemert, *First You Take a Pick and Shovel* (Lexington, Ky.: The John Bradford Press, 1979), p. 24.
5. Cooley, p. 15.
6. Valley I, pp. 60, 61, 66, 67, 69, 70, 73, 93.

7. Valley I, p. 93; Lemert, pp. 11, 12, 17, 18, 21.
8. Stephen E. Ambrose, "Nothing Like it in the World: The Men Who Built the Transcontinental Railroad 1863–1869" (New York: Simon and Schuster, 2000), pp. 160, 244. This tunneling technique, modified to include a vertical access shaft to provide four working faces, was used in 1866–1867 on the Central Pacific Railroad's construction of the 1,659-foot Summitt Tunnel.
9. Lemert, pp. 3–20.
10. Dixon Merritt, *Sons of Martha* (Mason and Hanger Company, Inc., Long Island City, N.Y.: J. F. Tarpley Company, 1928), pp. 99, 110; MacMaster, p. 66.
11. *Staunton Vindicator*, July 28, 1876; Valley I, pp. 93, 226, 227.
12. Lee A. Wallace, *Fifth Virginia Infantry* (Lynchburg, Va.: H. E. Howard Inc., 1988), p. 125.
13. 1870 Census, Augusta County, Va.; John M. Carroll, *List of Staff Officers of the Confederate States Army, 1861–1865* (Mattituck, N.Y. and Bryan, Tex.: J. M. Carroll Publishing Company, 1983), p. 111; MacMaster, p. 67.
14. 1870 and 1880 Census, Roanoke County, Va.; Carroll, p. 65.
15. 1870 Census, Allegheny County, Va.; Lemert, pp. 23, 24; Thomas W. Dixon Jr., "C&O Allegheny Subdivision," Alderson, W.Va.: The Chesapeake and Ohio Historical Society Inc., 1985, p. 11; Valley I, p. 398.
16. 1870 Census, Orange County, Virginia; Michael P. Musick, *Sixth Virginia Cavalry* (Lynchburg, Va.: H. E. Howard Inc., 1990), p. 135; Merritt, p. 113.
17. 1870 Census, Henrico County, Va.; Janet B. Hewitt, *The Roster of Confederate Soldiers, 1861–1865, Volume 10* (Wilmington, N.C.: Broadfoot Publishing Company, 1996); p. 238; Lemert, pp. 21, 23.
18. *Staunton Vindicator*, July 28, 1876.
19. 1850 Census, Hanover County, Va.; 1860 and 1870 Census, Louisa County, Va.
20. David F. Riggs, "13th Virginia Infantry," Lynchburg, Va.: H. E. Howard Inc., 1988, p. 116.
21. Valley I, p. 66.
22. James L. Randolph, "Chief Engineer's Report, year ending September 1, 1873".
23. George L. Vose, *Manual for Railroad Engineers* (Boston: Lee and Shepard Publishers, 1873), p. 79.
24. Randolph, Report for year ending September 1, 1873.
25. Valley I, p. 118.
26. Valley I, p. 128.
27. Valley I, p. 140.
28. Valley I, pp. 226, 227.
29. Valley I, pp. 195, 258.
30. Merritt, pp. 57, 194, 195.
31. MacMaster, p. 67.
32. Peter Way, *Common Labor, Workers and the Digging of North American Canals, 1780–1860* (Baltimore and London: The Johns Hopkins University Press, 1997), pp. 97, 133, 134, 142.
33. Way, p. 272. The caption on a photographic display in the B&O Railroad Museum in Baltimore, Maryland, provides an insight into the men who constructed 19th-century American railroads. The caption is titled "Hard Work," and reads as follows: "Following the civil engineers were the laborers. Using wheel barrows and horse drawn carts, they cut down trees, moved tons of stone, earth and a stubborn material referred to as indurated clay. These 'cart-men' worked 10 or more hours a day in all kinds of weather, sometimes straight through the night. Their reward was 50 cents a day, some whiskey and a bunk in a shanty or house car that sat at the end of the tracks. These unsung Irish, German, and African-American laborers were literally on 'the cutting edge of the frontier.'"

34. Joseph A. Waddell, "Annals of Augusta County Virginia, from 1726 to 1871" Staunton, Va., C. R. Caldwell, 1902, pp. 442, 443.
35. J. Randolph Kean, *The Development of the 'Valley Line' of the Baltimore and Ohio Railroad* (*Virginia Magazine of History and Biography*, October, 1952), pp. 539, 541.
36. Dixon, pp. 11, 22.
37. Lemert, p. 23.
38. Dixon, p. 15.
39. Valley I, p. 368.

Bibliography

BOOKS

Barnes, Raymond P. *A History of Roanoke*. Radford, Va.: Commonwealth Press Inc., 1968.

Brown, Stuart E., Jr. *Annals of Clarke County*. Berryville, Va.: Virginia Book Company, 1983.

Bushong, Millard A. *A History of Jefferson County, West Virginia*. Charles Town, W.Va.: Jefferson Publishing Company, 1941.

Carroll, John M. *List of Staff Officers of the Confederate States Army, 1861–1865*. Mattituck, N.Y. and Bryan, Tex.: J. M. Carroll Publishing Company, 1983.

Cooley, Thomas M. *American Railway—Its Construction, Development, Management, and Appliance*. New York: Charles Scribner's Sons, 1889.

Cooper, Mason Y. *Norfolk and Western's Shenandoah Valley Line*. Norfolk and Western Historical Society Inc., 1998.

Couper, William. *History of the Shenandoah Valley*. New York: Lewis Historical Publishing Company, 1952.

Davis, Burke. *The Southern Railway, Road of the Innovators*. Chapel Hill and London: The University of North Carolina Press, 1985.

Dixon, Thomas W., Jr. *C&O Allegheny Subdivision*. Alderson, W.Va.: The Chesapeake and Ohio Historical Society Inc., 1985.

Driver, Robert. *52nd Virginia Infantry*. Lynchburg, Va.: H. E. Howard Inc., 1986.

Freeman, D. S. *Robert E. Lee, A Biography, Volume IV*. New York: Charles Scribner's Sons, 1948.

Frey, Robert L., ed. *Encyclopedia of American Business History and Biography, Railroads in the Nineteenth Century*. New York and Oxford, Facts on File: A Bruccoli, Clark, Layman Book, 1988.

Hewitt, Janet B. *The Roster of Confederate Soldiers, 1861–1865, Volume 10*. Wilmington, N.C.: Broadfoot Publishing Company, 1996.

Hungerford, Edward. *The Story of the Baltimore and Ohio Railroad, 1827–1927*. New York and London: G. P. Putnam's Sons, the Knickerbocker Press, 1928.

Lemert, Ann Arnold. *First You Take a Pick and Shovel*. Lexington, Ky.: The John Bradford Press, 1979.

MacMaster, Richard K. *Augusta County History 1865–1950*. Staunton, Va.: Augusta County Historical Society, 1987.

Merritt, Dixon. *Sons of Martha*. New York: Mason and Hanger Company Inc., J. F. Tarpley Company, 1928.

Middleton, Norwood C. *Salem, A Virginia Chronicle*. Salem, Va.: Salem Historical Society Inc., 1986.

Moger, Allen W. *Virginia, Bourbonism to Byrd, 1870–1925*. Charlottesville, Va.: The University Press of Virginia, 1968.

Moody, John. *Railroad Builders, A Chronicle of the Welding of the States*. New York: United States Publishers Association, 1919.

Morris, Richard B., ed. *Encyclopedia of American History*. New York: Harper and Brothers, 1953.

Musick, Michael P. *Sixth Virginia Cavalry*. Lynchburg, Va.: H. E. Howard Inc., 1990.

Riggs, David F. *13th Virginia Infantry*. Lynchburg, Va.: H. E. Howard Inc., 1998.

Scharf, J. Thomas. *History of Western Maryland, being a history of Frederick, Montgomery, Carroll, Washington, Alleghany and Garrett Counties*. Baltimore Regional Publishing Company, 1968.

Stover, John F. *The Railroads of the South, 1865–1900, A Study in Finance and Control*. Chapel Hill, N.C.: The University of North Carolina Press, 1955.

Strickler, Harry M. *A Short History of Page County, Virginia*. Harrisonburg, Va.: C. J. Carrier, 1974.

Striplin, E. F. *The Norfolk and Western, A History*. Norfolk and Western Railway Company, 1981.

Summers, Festus S. *The Baltimore and Ohio in the Civil War*. New York: G. P. Putnam's Sons, 1939.

Vose, George L. *Manual for Railroad Engineers*. Boston, Mass.: Lee and Shepard, 1873.

Waddell, Joseph A. *Annals of Augusta County from 1726 to 1871*. Staunton, Va.: C. R. Caldwell, 1902.

Wallace, Lee A. *Fifth Virginia Infantry*. Lynchburg, Va.: H. E. Howard Inc., 1988.

Way, Peter. *Common Labor, Workers and the Digging of North American Canals, 1780–1860*. Baltimore and London: The Johns Hopkins University Press, 1997.

Wayland, J. W. *A History of Rockingham County*. Dayton, Va.: 1912.

Westhaffer, Paul J. *History of the Cumberland Valley Railroad, 1835–1919*. Washington, D.C. Chapter, National Railway Historical Society, 1979.

White, Clare. *Roanoke 1740–1982*. Roanoke Valley Historical Society, 1982.

Workers of the Writer's Program of the Works Project Administration in the State of Virginia. *Roanoke, Story of City and County*. American Guide Series, 1942.

NEWSPAPERS, PERIODICALS, AND PAMPHLETS

Harman, Thomas S. "The Secession Crisis in the Shenandoah Valley, How Staunch Unionists Became Ardent Confederates," unpublished.

Kean, J. Randolph. "The Development of the 'Valley Line' of the Baltimore and Ohio Railroad," *Virginia Magazine of History and Biography*, October 1952.

Moger, Allen W. "Railroad Practices and Policies," *Virginia Magazine of History and Biography*, October 1951.

Paxton, Matthew W., Jr. "Bringing the Railroad to Lexington, 1866–1883," Rockbridge Historical Proceedings X (1980–1989).

Staunton Vindicator, July 28, 1876.

Tompkins, Dr. E. P. "Sketch of the Valley Railroad," Rockbridge Historical Society Collection, Washington and Lee University, 1947.

———. "A Short Sketch of the Valley Railroad," manuscript.

Virginia Magazine of History and Biography, vol. 4, no. 4, April 1897, "Necrology, Robert Garrett."

MANUSCRIPTS AND COLLECTIONS

Annual Report of the Railroad Commissioner to the General Assembly of Virginia, "Valley Railroad Company Report, 1884."

Garrett, Robert. "First Valley Railroad Company Report to the Board of Public Works," Valley Railroad Minute Book, vol. 1, September 30, 1872.

————. "Second Valley Railroad Company Report to the Board of Public Works, 1872–1873."

Office of the Clerk of the Circuit Court, Rockbridge, Botetourt, and Roanoke Counties. "Grantee Records, 1872, 1873, and 1874."

Randolph, James L. "Chief Engineer's Report, year ending September 30, 1873." Valley Railroad Minute Book, vol. 1.

Roanoke Chapter, National Railway Historical Society. "Agreement, B&O Railroad Company, Valley Railroad Company and Roanoke and Southern Railway Company, July 11, 1890."

Roanoke County Clerk of the Circuit Court. "Deed Books L, M, 302 and Charter Book 1."

Shenandoah Valley Railway Company; Maryland and Washington Division of the Norfolk and Western Railroad. "A Corporate History," 1891.

Shenandoah Valley Railroad Company. "Stockholders' and Directors' Minute Book A, 1870–1881, and Minute Book B, 1881–1887." Special Collections Department of the University Libraries of Virginia Tech, Blacksburg, Va.

United States Census, Virginia; 1850—Hanover County; 1860—Louisa County; 1870—Alleghany, Augusta, Henrico, Louisa, Orange, Page, and Roanoke Counties; 1880—Roanoke County, Roanoke Public Library, Virginia Room.

————, West Virginia; 1870—Berkeley County.

Valley Railroad Company. "Director's Minute Books, Unnumbered Volume, April 1866–June 1871, Vol. 1, June 1871–December 1878 and Vol. 2, November 1879–December 1943," B&O Railroad Museum, Hays T. Watkins Research Library, Baltimore, Md.

The Virginia General Assembly. "Acts of Assembly, Sessions of 1866–1867 and 1869–1870," Roanoke Law Library, Roanoke, Va.

————. "Acts and Joint Resolutions passed by the General Assembly of Virginia, Sessions of 1872–1873, 1875–1876, 1878–1879 and 1879–1880."

Washington and Lee Web page. "History of Washington and Lee," "Heritage," 1995.

MAPS AND ILLUSTRATIONS

American Railway—Its Construction, Development, Management and Appliance, illustrations, "Engineers in Camp" and "Making an Embankment."

Department of the Interior, U.S. Geological Survey, Roanoke Quadrangle, 1:62,500, base map, "Alternate Routes from Shenandoah Valley mainline into Big Lick and Bonsack."

Frey, Robert S. "Building a Masonry Arch," two illustrations, 2000.

Hildebrand, John R. Map of "Virginia Railroads—1872," 1999.

Kayton, Douglas W. "Claibourne Rice Mason, 1810–1866, Railroad Builder and Founder of the Mason Syndicate," a portrait, 1998.

National Archives, Research Branch, "Survey of the Valley Railroad, Lexington to Salem, Valuation Section 21-VA-34.2," Interstate Commerce Commission, Bureau of Valuation, 1920.

United States Department of the Interior Geological Survey, "7.5 Minute Series (Topographic), Lexington, Glasgow, Natural Bridge, Arnold Valley, Buchanan, Salisbury, Montvale, Villamont, Daleville, Roanoke and Salem Quadrangles," base maps for locating the Valley Railroad.

Index

A

Allan, William, VRR director, 119 n. 2
Almond, Thomas M., SVRR director, 20
Armes, George R. W.
　secretary, Roanoke Machine Works, 43
　secretary, SVRR, 45
Atlantic, Mississippi, and Ohio Railroad
　financial condition, 25, 27
　organized, 11
　purchased by E. W. Clark Company, 16, 17, 36, 37

B

Baird, Matthew, SVRR trustee, 118 n. 56
Baldwin, John B., Staunton attorney, 51, 119 n. 14
Baldwin Locomotive Works, 36
Baltimore and Ohio Railroad
　Camden Station, 64
　expansion activities, 6, 7, 10–12, 49
　labor discord, 59, 66
　Mount Claire Shops, 79
　VRR sponsor and stockholder, 2, 7, 13, 49, 52, 54, 59
Baltimore city
　Board of Trade, 50
　City Council, 50
　Finance Committee, 61
　VRR stockholder, 53, 54, 59
Bardwell, George H., SVRR director, 20
Blackwell, Charles, SVRR superintendent of machine works, 45
Blair, Henry E., Roanoke County, 62
Borst, Peter B., SVRR president, 20, 21
Borst Construction Company, 33
Botetourt County supervisors, 57, 63, 64

Boyce, Upton L.
　biographic sketch, 26
　member, SVRR Committee on Construction, 37, 41
　Roanoke Machine Works director, 43
　SVRR director, 22, 24, 25
　SVRR vice president, 26, 28, 29, 33–36, 45
Boyd, James A., contractor, 64, 65
Brady, C. D. E., VRR director, 119 n. 2
Bureau of Valuation, Interstate Commerce Commission, 70, 73, 89

C

Cameron, Simon, United States senator, Pennsylvania, 12
Central Improvement Company, railroad contractor, 13, 16, 20, 22–25, 27, 33
Chesapeake and Ohio Railroad
　coal deposits found, 23, 54
　completed to Huntington, West Virginia, 22, 54
　organized, 47, 74
Chesapeake and Western Railway, 67
Christian, Bolivar, VRR director, 119 n. 2
Clark, Clarence W.
　E. W. Clark and Company president, 31, 36
　member, Committee on Construction, 37
　purchases SVRR, conveys to N&W, 46
　Roanoke Machine Works director, 43
　Shenandoah Valley Construction Co. officer, 32, 34
　SVRR director, 36
Clark, Edward W., 31
Clerk of Circuit Court, Roanoke County, 41, 42
Clark, Enoch W., 31
Clark, E. W. and Company, Philadelphia
　acquires AM&O, creates N&W, 36, 37
　SVRR sponsor, 17, 30, 31, 33, 35, 36, 45, 67

Clark, E. W., Jr., Roanoke Machine Works director, 43
Coe, W. W.
  Shenandoah Valley Construction Co. chief engineer, 36, 37
  SVRR chief engineer, 42, 45
Coffman, Dr. S. A., VRR director, 119 n. 2
Confrade Saylor Construction Company, 33
Cooke, Jay, 6, 24, 31
Coxe, Joseph W., SVRR auditor and general ticket agent, 45
Creveling, Alfred, railroad contractor, 28
Crozet, Cladius, civil engineer and railroad builder, 39, 74
Cumberland Valley Railroad, 7, 19, 22, 24, 25, 32

D

Dandridge, William F., VRR survveyor, 72, 73, 84
Dorman, J. B., Rockbridge County attorney, 60, 62
Dreher, Dr. Julius, Roanoke College president, 38
Durand, Joseph, SVRR solicitor, 45

E

East Tennessee, Virginia and Georgia Railroad, 7, 43
Echols, John, VRR director, 119 n. 2
Effinger, M. Harvey, VRR director, 119 n. 2

F

Farmers Loan and Trust Company, New York, 29
Fidelity Insurance Trust and Safe Deposit Company, Philadelphia,
  37
Fincastle, Botetourt County, macadamized road to, 57
Fink, Henry, AM&O receiver, 27
Fisher, Thomas, railroad historian, 87
Flickwir, D. W., 34

G

Garrett, John W., B&O president, 6, 8, 12, 49, 59, 66, 67
Garrett, Robert
  annual reports, 52, 53, 55
  biographic sketch, 51
  B&O president, 66
  VRR president, 17, 51, 54–57, 66, 73
Gooch, Garrett G., 78, 79
Gooch, Stapleton D., 78, 79, 84
Green, Joel C., 73, 75–77

H

Hansbrough, Colonel George W., Roanoke County, 62
Harman, Asher W., 48, 73, 75, 76, 84, 85
Harman, Michael G.
  biographic sketch, 47
  death, 59
  VRR director, 48
  VRR president, 17, 48, 50, 51, 76

Hoar, Samuel, SVRR director, 20
Hungerford, Edward, B&O historian, 67
Huntington, Collis P., founder, C&O Railroad, 6

J

James River bridge, between Pattonsburg and Buchanan,
  Botetourt County, 57, 63
Jamison, B. K., SVRR director and treasurer, 20, 28, 29
Jamison, S. M., Roanoke and Southern Railroad secretary, 66
Jollifee, William, VRR surveyor, 72, 73

K

Kennedy, Thomas B., Cumberland Valley and SVRR president,
  23, 25
Keyser, William, VRR president, 60–63, 65
Kimball, Frederick J.
  biographic sketch, 30
  E. W. Clark and Company partner, 31
  May 5, 1881, report, 38, 42
  Roanoke Machine Works president, 43
  Shenandoah Valley Construction Co. president, 31, 32, 36
  SVRR president, 17, 36, 39, 43, 45
Kimball, Frederick S., 32

L

Latrobe, Ferdinand, City of Baltimore Finance Committee
  chairman, 61
Lee, Robert E.
  accomplishments as Washington College president, 51
  letter accepting VRR presidency, 119 n. 14
  post Civil War activities, 51
  VRR president, 51
  VRR spokesman, 50

M

MacDowell, W. G., Roanoke Machine Works treasurer, 43
Mahone, William
  AM&O president, 6, 8, 25
  biographic sketch, 10
  creates Atlantic, Mississippi and Ohio Railroad, 11
  opposition to B&O and Pennsylvania Railroads, 11, 12, 15,
    21, 54
  United States senator, 38, 39
Manassas Gap Railroad, 48, 49
Martinsburg and Potomac Railroad, 29
Mason, Claibourne Rice
  as head of Mason Syndicate, 39, 73
  as head of Mason Syndicate, VRR construction, 76, 82–84
  biographic sketch, 74
Mason, H. P. and Brother, contractors, 76, 77, 84, 98
Mason, Horatio P., 73, 75, 77, 84

Mason, Silas B., 73, 75, 77, 78, 84
Mason and Hanger Company, 75
Mason and Shanahan, contractors, 60
Mason Syndicate, 53, 56–58, 60, 65, 72, 73, 75, 76, 79, 84–86
Mayer, Charles T., B&O and VRR president, 66
Mayo, Stephen Lacy, 119 n. 104
McDonald, A. W., SVRR director and stockholder, 33
McDonald, William G., SVRR treasurer, 35
McDowell, William J., SVRR treasurer, 45
McLellan, William M., SVRR president, 23-25
McMahon, Edward, 73, 75-77
McMahon and Green Company, contractors and VRR stock-
    holders, 52, 76, 79, 84, 91
Menifee, Thomas K., 73, 75, 76, 78, 82, 84, 100
Michie, Thomas I., 51, 119 n. 14
Mills and Rowland Construction Company, 32
Milnes, William, Jr.
    biographic sketch, 25
    member, Committee on Construction, 37
    owner, Shenandoah Iron Works, 16, 45
    SVRR director, 17, 20, 22, 24
    SVRR president, 25, 27-29, 33-36
    SVRR vice president, 25
Moomaw, John C., SVRR right-of-way agent, 2, 18, 39, 41, 42
Moomaw, Lucinda, 41
Morse, Forster, 34

N

National Security Iron, Coal and Improvement Co., contrac-
    tors, 58
Norfolk and Western (N&W) Railroad
    acquires SVRR, 46
    organized, 16, 17, 36, 37
    Winston-Salem division, 66

P

Page County Supervisors, 35, 43
Painter, William, SVRR director, 20
Panic of 1873, 17, 24, 25, 55-57, 61, 66
Patton, James T., VRR director, 119 n. 2
Pendleton, Edmund, VRR director, 119 n. 2
Pendleton, P. P., VRR president, 57, 60
Pennsylvania Railroad
    Baltimore-Washington branch line, 12
    expansion activities, 6, 7, 10-12
    participant, Southern Security Company, 21, 24
    SVRR sponsor and stockholder, 2, 7, 13, 21, 22, 25, 33, 45, 67
Potomac River Railroad Bridge, 11, 12

R

Railroad Equipment Company, 33

Railroad construction workers
    African Americans, 85-87
    convict labor, 58, 59, 87
    Henry, John, "steel driving man," 86
    Irish, 85-87
    May, Walker, Roanoke County stonecutter, 85, 86
    McKenny, Harry, Irish stonemason, 86
    slave labor, 86
Randolph, James L.
    B&O civil engineer and chief engineer, 49, 70
    biographic sketch, 70
    VRR chief engineer, 52, 53, 55, 72, 73, 79, 82-84
Richmond and Alleghany Railroad, 45, 63-65, 67, 84
Roanoke and Southern Railway Company, 66
Roanoke College, 16, 38
Roanoke County Supervisors, 50, 62
Roanoke Machine Works
    officers, 43
    organized, 24, 43
    purpose, 43, 45
Rockbridge County Supervisors, 60, 62, 63
Rockfish Gap tunnel, 39, 74, 86

S

Sands, Joseph, SVRR superintendent, 34, 45
Satterlee, John, railroad contractor and SVRR superintendent,
    28-30, 32
Scott, Thomas A.
    biographic sketch, 21
    Pennsylvania Railroad officer, 6, 8, 12, 13, 24-26, 43, 49
    SVRR president, 21-23
Shanahan, Dennis, 73, 75-77, 84, 94
Sheffey, Hugh, VRR counsel, 51, 119 n. 14
Shenandoah Valley Construction Company
    officers, 32
    organized, 30, 32
    SVRR contract, Hagerstown-Waynesboro, 30, 36, 37
    SVRR contract, Waynesboro-Big Lick, 36, 37
    SVRR stockholder, 33, 35
    VRR transfer, 64
Shenandoah Iron Works, 16, 31, 45
Shenandoah Valley Railroad
    capitalization, 19, 20, 21, 37
    charter, charter amendments (Va., W.Va., Md.), 19, 20, 32,
        33, 42
    Committee on Construction, 37, 38, 41, 42
    completed, 45
    construction, 28, 29, 32-36, 46
    conveyed to N&W, 46
    extension south from Waynesboro, 36, 37, 42, 43
    financing, 21, 22, 29, 32, 33, 35, 37

motive power and rolling stock, 33, 36, 46

operations, 29, 32, 35, 36, 45

planning, 27-29, 32

relations with local communities, 23, 27, 33, 35, 37

report to Virginia Railroad Commissioner, 45

traffic agreements and connection contracts, 23-27, 35, 37, 43

VRR lease, 18, 27, 28

Southern Security Company, 21, 24

Spencer, Samuel

biographic sketch, 65

VRR president, 17, 65

Spittler, Mann, SVRR director, 20

Strasburg and Harrisonburg Railroad, 49, 53, 67

Strayer, Dr. J. B., VRR director, 119 n. 2

Stuart, Alexander H. H., post-Civil War political leader, 51, 119 n. 14

T

Terry, Peyton L., Roanoke Machine Works director, 43

Thomas, Charles W. (C. M.), 2, 41

Thomson, J. Edgar

Pennsylvania Railroad president, 10, 24

SVRR trustee, 118 n. 56

Tompkins, Dr. E. P., 14, 17, 67

Travers, William H.

Roanoke Machine Works director, 43

SVRR director and counsel, 20, 33, 35, 45

SVRR trustee, 118 n. 56

Trout, H. S., Roanoke and Southern Railway Company president, 66

Trout, John, Roanoke County, 62

Tyler, George F., Roanoke Machine Works director, 43

Tyler, Sydney F., receiver, SVRR, 46

U

U.S. Geological Survey, 70, 89

V

Valley Railroad

capitalization and financing, 47, 49, 50, 52-55, 57, 59, 61, 63-66

charter, charter amendments (Va., Md.), 47, 48, 50, 57, 58, 62, 63

construction activities and costs, 52-59, 64, 66

division of assets, 60, 61

lease to SVRR, 58

operations, 55–57

organization, 47

planning, 49, 52, 53, 55

relations, local communities, B&O and Baltimore, 49, 60-62, 67

reports to Virginia Railroad Commissioner, 58, 61, 62, 64

suspension of work in 1874, 56

traffic agreements and connection contracts, 53, 54, 63–66

transfer to SVRR or Shenandoah Valley Construction Co., 64, 65

Virginia and Tennessee Railroad

becomes part of AM&O, 10

B&O interest, 11, 15

SVRR southern terminus, 7, 19

VRR southern terminus, 7, 49, 53, 54, 65, 103

Virginia Central Railroad, 47, 74, 86

Virginia General Assembly legislation, 3, 10, 11, 19, 24, 42, 43, 62, 63

W

Walker, Gilbert C., Virginia governor, 21

Walker, J. A., SVRR director, 20

Ward, Julian, VRR surveyor, 72, 73

Winchester and Potomac Railroad, 48, 49, 53

Winchester and Strasburg Railroad, 48, 49, 53

Word, W. E. M., VRR director, 119 n. 2

Wright, Uriel S., 26